INSPIRED

—BY—

KARBALA

MEANING & DIRECTION

A Collection of Sermons & Letters

GRAND AYATOLLAH
M.S. ALHAKEEM

TRANSLATION BY JALAL MOUGHANIA

THE
MAINSTAY
FOUNDATION

Inspired by Karbala: Meaning and Direction

Author: Grand Ayatollah Sayyid Muhammad Saeed al-Hakeem

Translator: Jalal Moughania

© 2025 The Mainstay Foundation

Printed in the United States.

ISBN: 978-1943393237

CONTENT

TRANSLATOR'S PREFACE

It is with immense reverence and responsibility that I offer this translation of *Inspired by Karbala: Meaning and Direction*, a seminal work by the late Grand Ayatollah Sayyid Muhammad Saeed al-Tabatabai al-Hakeem (may Allah sanctify his soul). This text is more than a guide to commemorative practice; it is a theological, ethical, and jurisprudential meditation on the legacy of Karbala—its causes, meanings, and enduring role in the religious consciousness of the Shīʿa Muslim community.

Grand Ayatollah al-Hakeem stands among the foremost jurists and religious authorities of the post-Saddam generation in Iraq. As a pillar of the Islamic Seminary in the Holy City of Najaf, his voice emerged as one of clarity and continuity amidst both oppression and transformation. His writings reveal a jurist deeply attuned to the historical sufferings of the Ahl al-Bayt (as), yet equally concerned with the needs and questions of contemporary believers. The present volume, curated from a range of public sermons, private correspondences, and legal responsa, offers rare insight into how a modern marjaʿ articulates both normative guidance and devotional sensibility in an age of religious pluralism, globalized media, and shifting communal structures.

I had the distinct honor of previously translating *The Marjaeya: A Candid Conversation*, a text in which Sayyid al-Hakeem outlines the foundational principles of Shī'ī religious authority—its responsibilities, limitations, and philosophical underpinnings. That work was a dialogue on the role of the marja', while this current text serves as a dialogue between the marja' and the mourning community of Husayn (a). Together, they form an indispensable complement: one grounding us in the epistemic structure of the ḥawza, the other illuminating its existential heart in the tragedy of Karbala.

What distinguishes this volume is the comprehensive range of themes it addresses. From theological foundations for mourning rituals to ethical admonitions for speakers and preachers; from jurisprudential questions on ritual forms to detailed advice on preserving the spiritual, moral, and intellectual integrity of the commemorative space—Sayyid al-Hakeem offers a framework for meaningful engagement with the Husayni legacy. He critiques reductionist interpretations of the uprising of Imam Husayn (a), challenges cultural distortions of mourning, and reminds us that the remembrance of Karbala is not a symbolic performance but a lived ethos—rooted in truth, sacrifice, and divine purpose.

The translation process was marked by a conscious effort to maintain fidelity to the original Arabic while rendering the text into accessible English. The Arabic prose of Sayyid al-Hakeem is at once juridical and evocative, a balance I have sought to preserve. In doing so, I have retained key Islamic terms in transliteration when necessary (e.g., marja', maqātil, 'azā', istihbāb), and included Qur'anic verses and hadith references in their appropriate scholarly form. Where idiomatic differences arose, clarifying parentheticals were sparingly used to preserve both the spirit and the substance of the author's thought.

This translation was prepared to be released during the sacred season of Muharram, a time in which the Muslim world turns its gaze toward Karbala—not merely as an event of the past, but as a moral call across generations. In that spirit, this text serves as a guidepost for students, scholars, preachers, and faithful mourners alike. It affirms that the sanctity of this remembrance lies not only in ritual observance, but in the renewal of ethical purpose, communal conscience, and theological clarity. Karbala was not a failure of politics; it was the triumph of moral clarity over historical betrayal. Its power lies not in spectacle, but in sincerity. Not in theatrical grief, but in faithful reform.

This project continues my broader effort to make the guidance of the Marja'iyya more accessible to English-speaking audiences—particularly those seeking clarity, rootedness, and spiritual direction in today's world. It is a continuation of a deep commitment to translating and transmitting the legacy of the Islamic Seminary of Najaf with fidelity, clarity, and reverence.

Any shortcomings, errors, or imprecisions in this work are entirely my own and in no way reflect the precision or integrity of the late Grand Ayatollah. I ask Allah (swt) for forgiveness, and I welcome correction and guidance from those more knowledgeable, in the hope that this work may be of benefit and accepted in sincerity.

NOTE ON USAGE AND SPELLING

In writing this book, I have elected to use more familiar English spellings for names of figures and subjects and have done so without diacritical marks. Thus, you will see Ali instead of 'Ali and Umar instead of 'Umar.

Furthermore, though "Koran" is often used in English works, I have elected to use the more proper spelling of "Quran" to differentiate between the *qaf* and *kaf* in the Arabic, which, if confused, could render different meanings of the word.

The reader should note that the supplication of *salawat* (a prayer asking God to send His peace and blessings upon Muhammad and the household of Muhammad) and salutations (peace be upon them) are usually recited at the mention of the Holy Prophet and his family. This is normally marked in elaborate calligraphy in Arabic text, or with (sawa), (as), or a similar mark in English text. The reader is encouraged to recite such prayers in their honor for the blessings of their mentioning.

It is worthy of note that I also relied on the English translation of Ali Quli Qara'i when citing the verses of the Holy Quran throughout this book, with minor adaptations.

I pray that these choices make the book more reader friendly to the intended audience, the English-speaking reader.

With prayers for the hastening of the reappearance of the Awaited Imam (aj).

Sincerely,

Jalal Moughania[1]

Dearborn, Michigan, USA

Muharram 1, 1447 AH | June 27, 2025

---

[1] Haj Jalal Moughania is a law professor, lawyer, lecturer, and author whose work explores the intersections of law, leadership, and Islamic thought. He teaches Islamic Law at Wayne State University and the University of Detroit Mercy. Moughania is the author of *Ali: The Elixir of Love, Husayn: The Saga of Hope,* and *Fatima: The Flower of Life.* He is the co-author of *The Pope Meets the Ayatollah: An Introduction to Shia Islam.*

ABOUT THE AUTHOR

His Eminence Grand Ayatollah Sayyid Muhammad Saeed al-Hakeem was born in the Holy City of Najaf in 1934 CE. His father, Ayatollah Sayyid Muhammad Ali al-Hakeem, was a prominent scholar of his time. The author grew under the tutelage of his father, who began to teach him the basic courses of Islamic disciplines before the age of ten.

Since his youth, His Eminence was known for his knowledge, moral standing, and piety. He was respected amongst his peers and teachers for his keen understanding of the religious disciplines and critical approach in discussion. He was always alongside his father in the gatherings of scholarly learning and intellectual discourse.

Grand Ayatollah Sayyid Muhammad Saeed al-Hakeem was given special attention by his maternal grandfather, Grand Ayatollah Sayyid Muḥsin al-Hakeem, who assigned his grandson the task of referencing the manuscripts of his renowned jurisprudential encyclopedia, *Mustamsak al-ʿUrwat al-Wuthqā*. In the course of reviewing the manuscripts, His Eminence would discuss the text with his grandfather. Through those sessions, he gained a great wealth of knowledge and showcased his understanding and skill in the Islamic disciplines.

During his time at the Islamic Seminary of Najaf, His Eminence studied under some of the most prominent scholars. Those scholars included his father, his maternal grandfather, Grand Ayatollah Sheikh Husayn al-Hilli, and Grand Ayatollah Sayyid Abulqasim al-Khoei.

At the age of thirty-four, after having spent more than two decades of his life in the pursuit of religious learning, he began offering *baḥth khārij* (advanced seminars) in the principles of jurisprudence. Two years later, he began offering advanced seminars in jurisprudence based on the books of al-Shaykh al-Aʿẓam Murtaḍā al-Anṣārī and his grandfather, Grand Ayatollah Sayyid Muḥsin al-Hakeem. Since then, His Eminence would continue to teach advanced seminars despite the challenges and obstacles he would face.

Along with his teachers and peers, the Grand Ayatollah was active in public affairs ever since he joined the seminary. He was amongst the group of scholars that supported Grand Ayatollah Sayyid Muhsen al-Hakeem in his movement against communist influences in Iraq. In 1963, Grand Ayatollah Sayyid Muhammad Saeed al-Hakeem signed the notable petition from the seminary that denounced President Abdul Salam Arif's attempt to impose communism in Iraq.

When the Baathist regime overthrew its predecessor and took control of Iraq, Grand Ayatollah al-Hakeem continued his activism against the state's dictatorial policies. Most notably, he would defy Baathist threats to execute anyone who would fulfill the ritual of walking toward the city of Karbala. Thus, the Grand Ayatollah became a target of the Baathist regime and was forced into hiding until the regime finally closed the case. Yet despite all the harassment and persecution, Grand Ayatollah al-Hakeem remained in Najaf and refused to escape the country. He saw the mass departure as a threat to the existence of Najaf's seminary, and so decided to stay in the city to ensure its continuity.

On May 9th, 1983, after the Hakeem family's refusal to support the Baathist regime during the Iran-Iraq war, many of the family's members were arrested, including the Sayyid himself. There, they faced constant interrogation and all kinds of torture. They were beaten with nightsticks and administered electric shocks, along with other torture methods. With no access to any medical assistance, disease and illness began to spread. Still, the family's fortitude was not broken, and they persevered.

Shortly after the mass imprisonment of the family, the Grand Ayatollah began offering classes in Quranic exegesis. He found no other books or sources for study in the Baathist prison system other than a worn copy of the Holy Quran. The wardens soon found out about his class and forced him to stop teaching. Nonetheless, religious discussions and commemorations continued in secrecy throughout the family's years of imprisonment. During those years, a total of sixteen members of the Hakeem family were executed by the regime.

In 1985, the remainder of the imprisoned members of the Hakeem family were moved to Abu Ghraib prison, which was a minimum-security prison at the time. There, the Grand Ayatollah found an opportunity to continue teaching the advanced seminars he had offered before imprisonment. Since most of the inmates with him were highly educated seminarians and students of his, he quickly seized the opportunity to expand on an educational curriculum.

Finally, on June 7, 1991, His Eminence and the remainder of the Hakeem family were released from prison. However, that did not mean an end to Baathist harassment. The Baathist authorities harassed him in an attempt to have him accept the title of an official "state-designated religious authority." He unequivocally refused such offers, asserting that religious authority is and must always be independent. As a result of his firm position, the Iraqi government imposed significant restrictions on the Grand Ayatollah. Amongst those restraints included a ban on publishing any of his books and scholarly work and broad restrictions on his travel.

After the passing of Grand Ayatollah Sayyid Abulqasim al-Khoei the following year, many scholars and seminarians petitioned Grand Ayatollah al-Hakeem to assume the obligations and duties of a Marja' – the religious authority to whom the believers refer in issues of law. In compliance with the repeated petitions of students and peers, he put forward his views on Islamic law and practice, thus becoming one of the distinguished religious authorities of the time. He continued his scholarly work, writing and teaching across the fields of Islamic disciplines.

Grand Ayatollah M.S. al-Hakeem passed away on September 3, 2021 CE, and was buried in the Shrine of Imam Ali (a). He was one of the leading contemporary religious authorities for Shia Ithnā 'Asharī Muslims worldwide.

PROLOGUE

In the name of Allah, the Most Gracious, the Most Merciful.

Praise be to Allah, the Lord of all worlds, and blessings and peace be upon our Master Muhammad and his pure family. May Allah deprive His mercy and grace from their enemies until the Day of Judgment.

إِنَّ اللَّهَ اشْتَرَىٰ مِنَ الْمُؤْمِنِينَ أَنْفُسَهُمْ وَأَمْوَالَهُم بِأَنَّ لَهُمُ الْجَنَّةَ ۚ يُقَاتِلُونَ فِي سَبِيلِ اللَّهِ فَيَقْتُلُونَ وَيُقْتَلُونَ ۖ وَعْدًا عَلَيْهِ حَقًّا فِي التَّوْرَاةِ وَالْإِنجِيلِ وَالْقُرْآنِ ۚ وَمَنْ أَوْفَىٰ بِعَهْدِهِ مِنَ اللَّهِ ۚ فَاسْتَبْشِرُوا بِبَيْعِكُمُ الَّذِي بَايَعْتُم بِهِ ۚ وَذَٰلِكَ هُوَ الْفَوْزُ الْعَظِيمُ

Indeed, Allah has purchased from the believers their lives and their properties [in exchange] for that they will have Paradise. They fight in the cause of Allah, so they kill and are killed. [It is] a true promise [binding] upon Him in the Torah and the Gospel and the Qur'an. And who is truer to his covenant than Allah? So rejoice in your transaction which you have contracted. And it is that which is the great attainment.[2]

---

[2] The Holy Quran, 9:111.

We offer our condolences, as we enter the sacred month of Muharram, the month of sacrifice and redemption for the sake of Islam to the greatest Prophet (sawa), to his oppressed family (as), and especially to the remnant of Allah on Earth and the Imam of the Age, Imam Al-Mahdi (may Allah hasten his noble reappearance).

We beseech Allah, the Most High, to grant us success and make us among the supporters and helpers of Imam al-Mahdi (aj) when Allah (swt) allows him to avenge the oppressed from their oppressors and fill the world with justice and equity, after being filled with oppression and injustice.

At this moment, we find ourselves in a season of great religious significance. These days encompass elements of faith, struggle, emotion, and history. In the past, during an era of oppression, tyranny, and the suppression of freedoms, we could not openly discuss these matters due to the regime's hostility towards the Ahl al-Bayt (as) and their Shia followers. However, now that the suffocating darkness of that regime has lifted, it is essential for us to talk about it. In this new era, believers have regained their freedom. They can now engage in activities that were long denied to them. Their determination and endurance allowed them to preserve many of these activities, despite the regime's cruelty and oppression. This often led to intense conflicts, bloody clashes and enormous sacrifices. The Shia community, accustomed to challenges and confrontations, has endured losses and made sacrifices throughout its history, all for the sake of calling people to God's path and following the teachings of the Ahl al-Bayt (as), denouncing the oppressors, exposing their actions, and rejecting their deviations and innovations.

May Allah, the Most High, appreciate and reward these faithful souls for their efforts and struggles. May He raise the ranks of those who came before us among them, connecting them to

their pure Imams (as). May He guide those who remain on this
path to continue engaging in these activities in the best and
complete manner. This is after Allah, the Most High, granted
them relief, subdued their enemies, and restored their freedom
after prolonged suffering and severe trials. Allah, the Mighty
and Majestic, speaks the truth when He says:

أَمْ حَسِبْتُمْ أَنْ تَدْخُلُوا الْجَنَّةَ وَلَمَّا يَأْتِكُمْ مَثَلُ الَّذِينَ خَلَوْا مِنْ قَبْلِكُمْ
مَسَّتْهُمُ الْبَأْسَاءُ وَالضَّرَّاءُ وَزُلْزِلُوا حَتَّى يَقُولَ الرَّسُولُ وَالَّذِينَ آمَنُوا مَعَهُ
مَتَى نَصْرُ اللهِ أَلَا إِنَّ نَصْرَ اللهِ قَرِيبٌ

*Do you think that you will enter Paradise while such
[trial] has not yet come to you as came to those who
passed on before you? They were touched by poverty and
hardship and were shaken until [even their] messenger
and those who believed with him said, 'When is the help
of Allah?' Unquestionably, the help of Allah is near.*[3]

He also says:

مِنَ الْمُؤْمِنِينَ رِجَالٌ صَدَقُوا مَا عَاهَدُوا اللهَ عَلَيْهِ فَمِنْهُمْ مَنْ قَضَى نَحْبَهُ وَمِنْهُمْ
مَنْ يَنْتَظِرُ وَمَا بَدَّلُوا تَبْدِيلاً

*Among the believers are men true to what they
promised Allah. Among them is he who has fulfilled his
vow [to the death], and among them is he who awaits
[his chance]. And they did not alter [the terms of their
commitment] by any alteration.*[4]

After considering all of this, it is appropriate for us to delve into
the following chapters.

---

[3] The Holy Quran, 2:214.

[4] The Holy Quran, 33:23.

THE SORROW OF THE SHIA HAS GENUINE ROOTS

The sorrow of the Shia for the martyrdom of Imam Husayn (as) – along with all the calamities faced by the Ahl al-Bayt (as), the observance of mourning rituals, and the immersion in these commemorations – is not a matter driven by fanaticism or contrarianism. Nor is it a mere tradition inherited from their forefathers, lacking divine sanction. Rather, these activities are deeply rooted in genuine religious foundations, supported by strong and compelling evidence. They engaged in these activities willingly, enduring hardships and sacrifices.

Just as they were compelled by clear evidence to follow the example of the Messenger of Allah (sawa), accept his teachings, and adhere to Ahl al-Bayt (as) and follow them in their religion, the Prophet and the Imams (as) also encouraged them – by their sayings and behaviors – to deal with these tragic events in this manner.

In both schools of thought in Islam, narrations of the Holy Prophet (sawa) telling of the tragedies that would befall his family are prevalent – especially the tragedy of his grandson Imam Husayn (as). The Prophet cried profusely when mentioning the hardships faced by the Ahl al-Bayt (as) before

those events even took place.[5] The same can be said about The
Commander of the Faithful (as).[6]

In fact, it is reported that all the prophets (as) wept for Imam
Husayn (as) throughout history.[7] The earth and the heavens
wept blood for him after his martyrdom, as narrated by both
Sunni and Shia sources.[8] It is even mentioned that all of
creation mourned his tragedy, in details we cannot list now.[9]

---

[5] See: *Kamil al-Ziyarat*, 127, *Musnad Ahmad*, 3:242, and *Majma' Al-
Zawa'id*, 9:881.

[6] The Book of Siffin, 140.

[7] Kamil al-Ziyarat, 137.

[8] Among them are what al-Tabari and others have narrated regarding
the weeping of the heavens for Imam Husayn (as). See: *Jami' al-Bayan*
by al-Tabari, 25:160, and *al-Jami' li Ahkam al-Quran*, 16:14. And
among them is what is reported from al-Zuhri that whenever a stone
was lifted in Jerusalem, they would find underneath it traces of blood.
Ibn Hajar said, "It was narrated by al-Tabarani, and its narrators are
trustworthy." See: *Majma' al-Zawa'id*, 9:199. And among them is what
has been mentioned about the lamentation of the jinn, which was
narrated by a group of them and recorded by al-Tabarani in *al-
Mu'jam al-Kabir*, 3:221. That is also mentioned in *Majma' al-Zawa'id*,
9:199, with a comment that its narrators are reliable. Furthermore,
Abu Janab al-Kalbi narrated, "I came to Karbala and said to a
nobleman from the Arabs there, 'I heard that you people hear the
lamentation of the jinn?' He replied, 'You will not find a free man or a
slave, but that he will inform you that he heard it.'" See: *Al-Bidaya
wa'l-Nihaya*, 8:217, *Tahdhib al-Kamal*, 6:441, and *Siyar A'lam al-
Nubala*, 3:216.

[9] *Kamil al-Ziyarat*, 179; Al-Bayhaqi narrated with his chain of
transmission from Abu Qubayl who said: "When Husayn ibn Ali (may

Sources regard Lady al-Zahraa (as) one of the Weepers,[10] owing to her profound grief for her father, the Messenger of Allah (sawa). Imam Zain al-Abidin (as) is regarded among the Weepers, as he mourned and cried for his father Imam Husayn (as) more than anyone else.[11] In a hadith attributed to him (as), he said,

$$إني لم أذكر مصرع بني فاطمة إلا خنقتني العبرة لذلك$$

I could never recall the martyrdom of the sons of Fatima (as) without being overwhelmed by sorrow.[12]

In a narration about him (as), from Imam al-Sadiq (as), he said,

$$وكان جدي إذا ذكره بكى حتى تملأ عيناه لحيته، وحتى يبكي لبكائه رحمة له من رآه$$

Whenever my grandfather remembered him [i.e. Imam Husayn (as)], his tears would flow so abundantly that they would soak his beard [and he would cry so much] that those who saw him cry would cry as wel...[13]

And in the narration of Abu Amarah al-Munshid, he said:

Allah be pleased with them both) was killed, the sun was eclipsed, and the stars appeared in the middle of the day." *Al-Sunan Al-Kubra*, 3:337.

[10] Al-Bakka'in, or the Weepers, are noble and pious individuals whose mourning surpassed that of the rest of humankind.

[11] *Al-Khisal*, 372.

[12] Al-Saduq, *al-Amali*, 402.

[13] *Kamil al-Ziyarat*, 168.

ما ذكر الحسين (ع) عند أبي عبد الله (ع) في يوم قط فرُئي أبو عبد
الله (ع) متبسما في ذلك اليوم إلى الليل

Whenever Imam Husayn ibn Ali was mentioned in the presence of Abu Abdullah Jafar ibn Muhammad (Imam al-Sadiq), Abu Abdullah would not be seen smiling that day until the night.[14]

Similarly, there are narrations indicating that all the Imams (as) would seize any opportunity to discuss these tragic events, cry over them, encourage others to do the same, and hold gatherings to remember them. There were numerous mourning ceremonies that they personally organized where poets came to recite elegies and remember the tragedies.

In a narration from Imam al-Sadiq (as), he said,

ولقد شققن الجيوب ولطمن الخدود الفاطميات على الحسين بن علي.
وعلى مثله تلطم الخدود وتشق الجيوب

Indeed, the Fatimi[15] women tore their collars and slapped their cheeks for Husayn ibn Ali. Surely, for one like him, cheeks should be slapped, and collars should be torn.[16]

It is also narrated that he said,

---

[14] Ibid, 214.

[15] Related to Lady Fatimah al-Zahraa (as), daughter of Prophet Muhammad (sawa).

[16] *Tahdheeb al-Ahkam*, 8:325.

إن البكاء والجزع مكروه للعبد في كل ما جزع، ماخلا البكاء والجزع على
الحسين بن علي فإنه فيه مأجور

*Indeed, crying and grieving are disliked for a servant in
all situations of distress, except for crying and grieving
for Imam Husayn ibn Ali (as), for he will be rewarded
for that.[17]*

In his long and heartfelt supplication for the pilgrims visiting
Imam Husayn (as), Imam al-Sadiq (as) said:

اللهم إن أعداءنا عابوا عليهم بخروجهم، فلم ينهم ذلك عن الشخوص إلينا
خلافاً منهم على من خالفنا، فارحم تلك الوجوه التي غيرتها الشمس ...
وارحم تلك الصرخة التي كانت لنا

*O' Allah, our enemies criticized them for traveling [to
visit us], joining us, but that did not deter them from
coming to us, in opposition to those who opposed us. So
have mercy on those faces touched by the sun's heat...
and have mercy on those voices that cried in agony for
us...[18]*

In a narration, after describing his grief for Imam Husayn (as),
a man named Misma' Kirdin al-Basri was told by Imam al-
Sadiq (as),

رحم الله دمعتك، أما أنك من الذين يعدّون من أهل الجزع لنا، والذين
يفرحون لفرحنا، ويحزنون لحزننا، ويخافون لخوفنا، ويأمنون إذا أمنا، أما
أنك سترى عند موتك حضور آبائي ووصيتهم ملك الموت بك، وما

---

[17] *Kamil al-Ziyarat*, 201.

[18] Ibid, 228.

يلقونك به من البشارة أفضل، وملك الموت أرق عليك وأشد رحمة لك من الأم الشفيقة على ولدها.

May Allah have mercy on your tears. You shall be
counted among those who grieve for us, those who
rejoice in our joy, grieve in our sorrow, fear when we
fear, and feel secure when we feel secure. Know that
when you are about to die, you will see my forefathers
and they will instruct the Angel of Death [to be easy]
with you. What they will convey to you of glad tidings
will be even better. The Angel of Death will treat you
more gently and mercifully than a compassionate
mother to her child.

Kardin said, "He cried, and I cried as well." The Imam then said,

الحمد لله الذي فضلنا على خلقه بالرحمة، وخصنا أهل البيت بالرحمة

All praise is due to Allah, who has elevated us above
His creation by making their compassion and
lamentation directed toward us, and has set us – the
Ahl al-Bayt – apart through this distinctive response of
mercy...[19]

In a narration attributed to Imam al-Ridha (as), narrated by al-Rayyan ibn Shabib, he said,

يا ابن شبيب إن سرّك أن تكون معنا في الدرجات العلى من الجنان فاحزن لحزننا، وافرح لفرحنا، وعليك بولايتنا فلو أن رجلًا أحبّ حجراً لحشره الله عزّ وجلّ معه يوم القيامة

O' son of Shabib, if it pleases you to be with us in the highest ranks of Paradise, then grieve for our grief and rejoice in our joy. Embrace our guardianship, for if a person loves a stone, Allah will resurrect him with it on the Day of Judgment.[20]

The narrations from the Ahl al-Bayt (as), mentioned:

رحم الله شيعتنا خلقوا من فاضل طينتنا، وعجنوا بماء ولايتنا، يفرحون
لفرحنا ويحزنون لحزننا

May Allah bless our Shia; they were created from the remainder of our clay, molded with the water of our guardianship. They rejoice in our joy, grieve in our sorrow...[21]

There are countless more similar narrations. Many books have been dedicated to collecting and elaborating on these narrations, making it easier for people to learn about them.

It is the duty of the followers of Ahl al-Bayt, indeed of all Muslims, to be aware of the vast treasure of narrations and traditions regarding these matters. Especially now, with the accessibility and ease of learning through modern printing, publishing, and technology, they should gain a deeper understanding of these realities. They must recognize that they have not yet fulfilled, nor are they fulfilling, the due rights of these teachings, no matter how much effort they put into it.

---

[20] *'Uyun Akhbar Al-Rida*, 2:269.

[21] *Shajarat Touba*, 1:3.

THE IMMENSITY OF THE TRAGEDIES OF AHL AL-BAYT

If you take an objective and non-partisan view of these tragic events, it is sufficient to move the Muslim person to engage and immerse their self in the remembrance of these events.

This is because the Ahl al-Bayt are not ordinary individuals; rather, they represent the pinnacle of sanctity, purity, self-elevation, devotion to Allah, and striving in His cause. This is evidenced by what has been relayed in the Holy Quran and the countless hadiths from both Sunni and Shia sources.

Allah, the Most High, has commanded this nation to hold fast to them, refer to them, and align themselves with them. He has made them a source of safety from misguidance, deviation, division, and discord. He has mandated their love and affection.[22]

Furthermore, Allah has honored them with their position in relation to the Prophet, the guide and the savior for this nation, and the bearer of the highest proof upon it. They are from the Prophet (sawa), and he is from them. He is content with what pleases them and displeased with what displeases them. Their

---

[22] *Fi Rihab al-'Aqidah,* 1:224.

peace is his peace, their conflict is his conflict, their friend is his friend, and their enemy is his enemy.[23]

The Holy Prophet (sawa) would show them the greatest expressions of love, affection, honor, and reverence that words cannot fully describe. He would advise his Ummah regarding them, emphasizing the importance of preserving and upholding their rights.

However, the oppressors disregarded all of this and considered it insignificant, turning a blind eye to the sanctity of the Ahl al-Bayt and the sanctity of the Prophet (sawa) regarding them. They committed horrendous crimes in oppressing, killing, confining, looting, imprisoning, displacing, and expelling them, with extreme cruelty. They violated their sanctity and stopped at nothing in their pursuits. These tragedies are further compounded by the following:

DISTORTION BY THE OPPRESSORS

Firstly, the oppressors and their followers attempted to legitimize these crimes and transgressions. They manufactured excuses and justifications, and they opened the door to religious interpretation to distort the facts, ignoring the compelling evidence contrary to their interpretations. This led to outrageous claims about the tragedy of Karbala, stating that Imam Husayn (as) was killed by the sword of his grandfather (sawa).[24] It even reached the point where the Day of Ashura was declared a festive occasion in many Muslim lands.

---

[23] Ibid, 2:199.

[24] Al-Munawi stated in *Fayd al-Qadir*: "Ibn al-Arabi's inclination towards the disapproval of Ahl al-Bayt prevailed to the extent that he even claimed, 'He [Yazid] killed him [Imam Husayn (as)] with the

THE CAUSE OF THE TRAGEDIES OF AHL AL-BAYT

Secondly, what befell the Ahl al-Bayt (as) was due to the deviation of leadership and authority in Islam away from the right path Which Allah ordained to preserve His religion and establish justice in His lands. This deviation, from which Muslims suffer to this day, has led them away from the true path of Islam, and to disregarding its limits and judgments, departing from its morals and ethics, differing in their religion, fragmenting, dividing, striking one another, weakening and humiliating themselves, and allowing their enemies to dominate... and much more that, which does not require further elaboration.

THE ASCETICISM OF AHL AL-BAYT

Thirdly, Ahl al-Bayt (as), despite being the rightful authorities and having every right to claim their due, did not confront the oppressors to reclaim their rights out of worldly desires or a thirst for power and authority. Instead, they did so for the greater good of Islam and the Muslims, to preserve the boundaries and judgments of Allah, reform His servants, and establish justice in their lands. This is abundantly evident in their sayings and their conduct.

---

sword of his grandfather [Prophet Muhammad (sawa)]." In another context, al-Munawi wrote, "And this is not the first instance of audacity, shamelessness, and presumptuousness on the part of [Ibn al-Arabi]. He authored a book concerning our master Husayn (may Allah be pleased with him and honor him), and he disgraced himself by suggesting that Yazid rightfully killed him with the sword of his grandfather. We seek refuge in Allah from such shame." Al-Munawi, *Fayd al-Qadir*,1:265 and 5:213.

The Commander of the Faithful (as) supplicated, saying,

اللهم إنك تعلم أنه لم يكن الذي كان منّا منافسة في سلطان، ولا التماس
شيء من فضول الحطام، ولكن لنرد المعالم من دينك ونظهر الإصلاح
في بلادك، فيأمن المظلومين من عبادك، وتقام المعطلة من حدودك

*O' Allah, You know that our aim was not to compete
for authority, nor to seek any surplus from the spoils.
Rather, it was to restore the landmarks of Your religion
and promote reform in Your lands, so that the
oppressed among Your servants are secure, and the
limits of Your laws are upheld.*[25]

Imam Husayn (as) said in his instructions to his brother
Muhammad ibn al-Hanafiya,

وإني لم أخرج أشراً ولا بطراً، ولا مفسداً ولا ظالماً، وإنما خرجت
لطلب الإصلاح في أمة جدي (ص)، أريد أن آمر بالمعروف وأنهى عن
المنكر، وأسير بسيرة جدي، وأبي علي بن أبي طالب. فمن قبلني بقبول
الحق فالله أولى بالحق، ومن ردّ عليّ هذا أصبر حتى يقضي الله بيني
وبين القوم بالحق، وهو خير الحاكمين

*I do not revolt due to discontent, nor out of arrogance. I
did not rise as a corruptor, nor as an oppressor. Rather,
I wish to call for reform in the nation of my grandfather
(sawa). I wish to call for what is good, and to forbid
what is evil. [I wish to] follow the tradition of my
grandfather [the Prophet] and my father Imam Ali ibn
Abi Talib. Whoever accepts me by accepting the truth,
God is the best knower of the truth. Whoever rejects*

---

[25] *Nahj al-Balaghah*, 2:13, sermon 131.

*me, I shall be patient until God passes judgment
between me and them. He is the best Judge.*[26]

In his sermon to his companions when they arrived at Karbala,
Imam Husayn (as) said,

أَلَا تَرَوْنَ إِلَى الْحَقِّ لَا يُعْمَلُ بِهِ وَإِلَى الْبَاطِلِ لَا يُتَنَاهَى عَنْهُ، لِيَرْغَبِ
الْمُؤْمِنُ فِي لِقَاءِ اللهِ...

*Do you not see that the truth is not acted upon, and
falsehood is not abandoned? The believer should yearn
to meet Allah...*[27]

And as such there are numerous statements from them, as well
as what is well-known from the reality that they experienced.

In contrast, the behavior and statements of their adversaries
were characterized by a spirit of arrogance, pretension,
exploitation, injustice, recklessness, and the worst forms of
conduct. This is so apparent from history and is clearer than
needing further explanation.

The reality was that they had different paradigms and pursuits.
Due to differing objectives, the means also differed. The
immaculate nature and noble character were evident in the
methods of the Ahl al-Bayt (as), while others resorted to
recklessness, exploitation, deceit, and trickery, among other
manifestations of moral decline.

When certain people refused to pledge allegiance to The
Commander of the Faithful (as), he left them and their affairs,

---

[26] *Bihar al-Anwar*, 44:329.

[27] *Tarikh Dimashq*, 14:217.

unlike others who would have forced them into allegiance.
Imam Ali (as) said,

قد يرى الحُوّل القُلّب وجه الحيلة ودونها حاجز من تقوى الله فيدعها
رأي العين، وينتهز فرصتها من لا حريجة له في الدين

*The cunning alterant may see the opportunity for
deception, but before it is a deterrent for the adherence
to the command or prohibition of God. He will
disregard (this opportunity) though he sees it and has
the ability to take it. On the other hand, the
opportunity will be seized by one who is not restricted
by faith.*[28]

Imam Ali (as) was exceptional. He refused to seek victory
through unjust means, even if it means that leaders and chiefs
unite against him with their wealth. He would say,

أتأمروتني أن أطلب النصر بالجور فيمن وليت عليه؟! لا والله لا أطور
به ما سمر سمير وما أمّ نجم في السماء نجماً

*Do you command me to seek victory through
oppression over those under my authority? By God,
never—not as long as days turn and stars remain in the
sky.*[29]

When Muslim ibn Aqeel (as), the ambassador of Imam Husayn
in Kufa, was asked about his reason for abstaining from
assassinating Ubaidullah ibn Ziyad in the house of Hani ibn

[28] *Nahj al-Balaghah*, 1:92, sermon 41.

[29] Ibid, 2:6, sermon 126.

Urwah, he excused himself by referring to the narration of
Imam Ali (as) from the Prophet Muhammad (sawa):

إن الإيمان قيد الفتك، فلا يفتك مؤمن

*Faith is a restraint against assassination, and thus a
believer does not assassinate.*[30]

When Imam Husayn (as) intended to leave for Iraq, he
addressed the people in Mecca and informed them of his
inevitable destiny. He said,

ألا ومن كان فينا باذلاً مهجته موطّناً على لقاء الله نفسه فليرحل معنا

*Whoever is willing to sacrifice their life for us and is
prepared for meeting God, then let them depart with
us...*[31]

Similarly, when he received news, while he was on the way to
Karbala, of the murders of Muslim ibn Aqeel, Hani ibn Urwah,
and Abdullah ibn Yaqtur, and people's abandonment of them.
He gathered his followers, having been joined by many after
leaving Mecca, and informed them of these developments. He
allowed anyone who wished to leave to do so. Consequently,
people dispersed, and only those who had set out with him
from Mecca remained.[32]

All of this is because Imam Husayn (as) did not want to deceive
or force people. Instead, he wanted them to know fully what
they were getting themselves into. His message is directed

---

[30] *Tarikh al-Tabari*, 4:271.

[31] *Kashf al-Ghummah*, 2:239.

[32] *Tarikh al-Tabari*, 4:300; *Al-Bidaya wa'l-Nihaya*, 8:281.

towards those among them who have insight and who have prepared themselves for facing death and other such immaculate stands.

In contrast, their adversaries are quite the opposite, as has become evident without needing much explanation. It suffices to mention Muawiyah's speech when he entered Kufa: "I have not fought you so that you pray, fast, perform Hajj, or give Zakat. I know that you would do all of that. But I fought you so that I can dictate my orders upon you, and God has granted me that power, even if you dislike it."[33]

He openly stated about the peace terms he offered to Imam Hasan (as): "Everything that I have given to Hasan ibn Ali is under my feet, and I will not comply."[34]

Hence, the true struggle lies between truth, religion, and uprightness on one side and falsehood, deviation, and depravity on the other. The tragedies and oppression faced by the Ahl al-Bayt (as) are struggles for truth, faith, and morality, all of which have bene transgressed upon.

Therefore, it is the right of the Ahl al-Bayt (as) to be those form whom God will take His retribution, to seek vengeance for the sake of God, as stated in the Ziyarah of Imam Husayn (as):

السلام عليك يا ثار الله وابن ثاره والوتر الموتور

---

[33] *Al-Bidaya wa'l-Nihaya*, 8:410; *Tarikh Dimashq*, 59:150.

[34] Maqatil al-Talibiyyin, p. 45.

Peace be upon you, O' God's retribution, and the son of God's retribution, the unique one killed in the way of God.[35]

These are the motivations and justifications for the Shia position regarding the adversities, calamities, and tragedies that befell the Ahl al-Bayt (as), and their response to them. I do not think that any fair-minded person would blame them for their actions in light of these circumstances.

---

[35] *Kamil al-Ziyarat*, p. 328.

GUIDELINES FOR THE BELIEVERS

We have emphasized on various occasions the importance of commemorating the noble figures from the Ahl al-Bayt (as) by visiting their sacred shrines and commemorating the anniversaries of their births and martyrdoms. We have discussed this in our messages to the Iraqi people following the fall of the previous regime.

Now, it is time for the believers to exercise their freedom in engaging in various activities and expressing their fervent emotions towards the Ahl al-Bayt (as), especially during this significant season – the season of the outcry for the Ahl al-Bayt (as) during their great tragedy and epic battle, colored with their pure blood.

However, while we encourage these activities and stress their importance, we would like to draw the attention of the believers to the following points:

BEWARE OF THE SCHEMES OF ENEMIES

Firstly, the believers should be vigilant against the plots and mischief of enemies and corrupters who exploit people and engage in destructive actions, resulting in the harm of many innocent individuals. Believers, in general, should not become so engrossed in these activities or interact with them in a way that blinds them to any ulterior motives, which lets the corrupters to spread them and penetrate their society, allowing them to achieve their criminal aims. Thus, they should remain cautious, alert, and disciplined, and use all of their energies to observe the actions of the corrupters and track them. They should collaborate with the responsible authorities to maintain security and stability while placing their trust in God. They should seek His guidance and protection through the blessings of the Ahl al-Bayt (as), praying that He keeps them steadfast, surrounded with His care and attention, safeguards them against the harm of oppressors, and returns the schemes of aggressors and transgressors against themselves. He is indeed compassionate and merciful towards the believers, and He suffices as a guardian and an advocate.

FEEL THE UNITY OF PURPOSE

Secondly, when engaging in these blessed activities, the believers should feel a sense of unity in purpose and the sanctity of their objective due to their affiliation with the Ahl al-Bayt (as), who represent the pinnacle of perfection and devotion to God. This should serve as a motivating factor for them to unite their voices, strengthen their bonds of love and brotherhood, and overlook any unintentional mistakes that may arise from some of them.

They should rise above boasting, pride, competition, and discord, as Satan may try to introduce these elements into their minds, aiming to disrupt their noble work, diminish their rewards, divide their voices, and scatter their unity. They should seek refuge in God from the plots, evil, temptations, deceit, arrogance, and turmoil of Satan. Allah (swt) says:

إِنَّ الشَّيْطَانَ لَكُمْ عَدُوٌّ فَاتَّخِذُوهُ عَدُوًّا إِنَّمَا يَدْعُو حِزْبَهُ لِيَكُونُوا مِنْ أَصْحَابِ السَّعِيرِ

Indeed, Satan is to you a clear enemy. So take him as an enemy; he only invites his party to be among the companions of the Blaze.[36]

PRESERVING THE RELIGIOUS CHARACTER

Thirdly, the believers should maintain the religious and spiritual essence of these activities by upholding Allah's boundaries, observing their religious duties at the appointed times, displaying good character, safeguarding their speech, speaking truthfully, and adhering to other actions that align with the sanctity of these events and their connection to the Ahl al-Bayt (as).

These activities often encounter opposition from various quarters, including enemies and disruptors who diligently work to hinder them. When these enemies cannot prevent these rituals by force, they attempt to exploit any missteps, propagate false narratives, and magnify unfortunate incidents to discourage participation, in a way that can lead to justifications for restricting or curtailing these activities.

Therefore, it is our hope that the believers will conduct themselves with discipline, prudence, and exemplary behavior when engaging in these events. Allah (swt) says:

وَالَّذِينَ جَاهَدُوا فِينَا لَنَهْدِيَنَّهُمْ سُبُلَنَا وَإِنَّ اللَّهَ لَمَعَ الْمُحْسِنِينَ

---

[36] The Holy Quran, 35:5.

*As for those who struggle in Our cause, We will surely
guide them along Our Way. And Allah is certainly with
the good-doers.*[37]

FOCUS ON THE NOBLE OBJECTIVE

Fourthly, as the main purpose of these activities is to express
love and loyalty to the Ahl al-Bayt (as), fulfill their rights, and
empathize with them in their joys and sorrows, it is vital for the
believers to concentrate on this noble objective and never lose
sight of it.

If a member of the Shia wishes to innovate or rejuvenate aspects
of these activities, such as introducing new roles in poetry
recitation or unveiling banners and so on, they should ensure
that their creativity and innovation serve this primary goal and
focus on it. Their primary concern should not be artistic
creativity or innovation that might stray from this objective.
Otherwise, they risk deviating from the purpose and indulging
in frivolity, arrogance, and other distractions.

If one wishes to find self-assurance that their activities have the
desired objective, they should reflect on their state of mind;
when they imagine one of the immaculates,[38] such as Lady
Fatima al-Zahra (as) or the Awaited Imam (may Allah hasten

---

[37] The Holy Quran, 29:69.

[38] Twelver Shia Muslims believe that prophets and the Imams of Ahl
al-Bayt (as) are granted the blessing of *'ismah* – a 'blessing such that
they have no occasion to disobey a divine command or commit a sin,
despite their ability to do so' – see: Ibn al-Mutahhar al-Hilli, *al-Bab al-
Hadi 'Ashar*, 41–42. They are capable of sinning, but they choose not
to. This quality is what we refer to as their 'immaculacy,' but may also
be translated as 'infallibility.'

his reappearance), is participating in spirit. Let them ask themselves: are their creative efforts appropriate in the presence of these revered figures (as) or not? Even if these figures (as) are not physically present, they remain aware of the activities and actions of their Shia, overseeing them.

Above all, they should consider the role of Imam al-Mahdi (may Allah hasten his reappearance), because, according to numerous narrations, the deeds of the Shia are seen by Prophet Muhammad (sawa) and by him.[39] Therefore, they should choose what is most suitable in accordance with their guidance, closer to their satisfaction, and more likely to involve them. Allah, the Exalted, encompasses all, and He is the All-Watchful Witness over everything.

---

[39] *Al-Kafi*, 1:219.

GUIDANCE FOR PREACHERS AND SPEAKERS

The Shia of the Ahl al-Bayt (may Allah elevate their status) possess unique cultural gatherings, thanks to their Imams' (as) blessings and guidance. These gatherings are held frequently during occasions related to the Ahl al-Bayt's (as) births, celebrations, martyrdoms, and sorrows. The Shia dedicate immense material and spiritual efforts to these gatherings.

These gatherings are characterized by their voluntary nature, drawing individuals who participate out of religious ties, coupled with deep veneration and emotional attachment rooted in their loyalty to the Ahl al-Bayt (as). Consequently, they engage actively with these gatherings and the educational content presented therein, which is tailored to suit these occasions.

Therefore, it is imperative that they reap the appropriate benefits from these events in terms of religious education and emotional bonding with their principles and revered figures, who epitomize perfection, sanctity, self-sacrifice for the sake of Allah, and devotion to His cause. These gatherings should not be reduced to mere formalities or unproductive speeches, as this could be a waste of effort and would deviate from the lofty objectives for which these gatherings were established.

One of the most significant occasions among these events is the tragic event of Karbala. It is distinguished by the immense sacrifices offered by the Master of Martyrs and the select members of his family and companions (as). They dyed the land of Karbala with their pure blood, accompanied by a legacy of resilience, dignity, high moral standards, and noble character. In contrast, their adversaries displayed greater injustice, tyranny, cruelty, harshness, moral degradation, and a descent into abysmal depths.

As such, the holy month of Muharram holds immense importance for the Ahl al-Bayt (as) and their followers – the Shia. It rejuvenates their lofty principles, revitalizes the vigor of those principles across ages and generations, allows their voices to be heard worldwide as they stand up for truth and denounce falsehood, shouting against oppression and tyranny.

In this sacred season, preachers and speakers[40] (may Allah guide them) should make the people of this beloved country [i.e., Iraq] aware of their responsibilities in these critical circumstances. They should encourage active participation and caution against potential exploitation or suppression of their rights, and to maintain the unity of their words and intentions.

Regarding their educational and communicative role in the occasions dedicated to the Ahl al-Bayt (as), and especially

---

[40] *Muballigh*, or preacher, is an individual who spreads the teachings of Ahl al-Bayt (as) through lectures, sermons, and other forms of religious education. *Khatib*, or speaker, is a *muballigh* who incorporates rhetorical and poetic elements into their sermons, such as elegies of the Ahl al-Bayt (as).

during these events, it is incumbent upon them to observe the following.

EDUCATING ON RELIGIOUS JURISPRUDENCE

Firstly, speakers and preacher should seek avenues to educate the believers about their religion, acquainting them with the intricacies of religious laws and its details. This is crucial due to the general need of the faithful for such knowledge and its significance in practical religious life. Without continuous education and focused awareness campaigns, access to and understanding of these matters would be limited.

This matter becomes even more important in this beloved country due to the enormous gap resulting from the previous regime's long-standing positions. The regime deliberately waged a systematic war against religious education, attempting to uproot it entirely. Were it not for Allah's care and protection, it might have succeeded.

EMPHASIS ON THEOLOGICAL ASPECTS

Secondly, speakers and preachers should emphasize the theological dimension, particularly regarding the exalted status of the Ahl al-Bayt (as) in the eyes of Allah. They should delve into what has been mentioned about them in the noble Quran and the noble Prophetic Sunnah. They should highlight the historical evidence of their unwavering commitment to the truth, adherence to moral ideals, and rejection of injustice and falsehood. This should be accompanied by highlighting the wretchedness of their adversaries; their aggression, heinous crimes, and their reprehensible lives and behaviors.

This approach has a significant impact on engaging the minds, hearts, and emotions of the people, directing them towards the Ahl al-Bayt (as) and their noble principles, fostering a strong connection with them. It also instills a deep aversion to oppression, oppressors, and their followers, leading to their condemnation. All of this is an integral part of sound belief.

And although the believers are generally aware of this, many of them remain heedless of the details and the evidence supporting it. Therefore, it is imperative that they [i.e., the believers] delve into the specifics and internalize the evidence, thus enhancing their insight into their religion. This will equip them with immunity against the waves of skepticism and opposition, as those who promote these notions possess significant media capabilities that make countering them challenging.

FOCUSING ON THE THEIR CALAMITIES

Thirdly, there should be a focus, especially from the speakers, on the sufferings and tribulations of the Ahl al-Bayt (as), highlighting the cruelty inflicted upon them. They must express grief through various forms of speech, whether in prose or poetry, in order to evoke emotions and draw tears, dedicating a portion of the lecture and discourse to this purpose.

This approach has the most significant impact in drawing people towards the Ahl al-Bayt (as) and distancing them from their enemies. Our Imams (as) have emphasized this through their words and actions in an astonishing manner, leaving no room for doubt or excuse. We cannot possibly cover all that has been reported from them on this topic because it goes beyond enumeration.

The speaker should make use of the available narrations and accounts according to the context and audience, as this can be more effective in invoking grief and tears, fostering a sense of connection and empathy with them (as).

EMPHASIZING THE USE OF QURAN AND SUNNAH AS REFERENCES

Fourthly, an attempt should be made to connect the information presented by the preacher or speaker in matters of belief, education, and emotions with what is mentioned in the Holy Quran and the traditions of the Prophet and his Ahl al-Bayt (as). This enables the listener to feel that they are receiving knowledge from the original and pure sources, not mere conjectures, personal opinions, or imitation lacking divine authority. This approach has the most profound impact in settling the hearts with the knowledge being conveyed by the speaker – drawing people toward it, engraving it in their minds, and fostering their engagement with it.

Rather, a speaker should enrich their lectures with abundant references to Qur'anic verses, as well as the sayings, supplications, and sermons of the Prophet and his Ahl al-Bayt (as), drawing from their hadith, speeches, and duʿas. This is not merely for the purpose of supporting the discussion but also to captivate the listeners' attention and encourage them to engage with the speaker. These noble texts are distinguished by their sanctity and spirituality, eloquence, strength and depth, grandeur and beauty, and radiance and brilliance.

As a result, they almost serve as a miracle that testifies to the elevated status of those who spoke them (as) and the magnitude of their importance. They also become a badge of honor for their Shia and devotees, setting them apart and bearing witness to their allegiance. In truth, their sincere affiliation with the Ahl al-Bayt (as) and their pride in drawing from them is apparent. The Ahl al-Bayt (as) bestowed this knowledge upon their Shia and devotees, entrusting them with it. They, in turn, nurtured it, safeguarded it, and diligently worked to preserve it, spread it, and acquaint people with it.

THE CAUSES OF THE HUSAYNI RENAISSANCE

Among scholars and historians from both groups,[41] there is a common practice of presenting and discussing the tragic event of the Battle of Karbala. They have two main approaches in doing so:

PLANNING FOR THE RENAISSANCE AS A HUMAN ENDEAVOR

The first approach is that the planning for this event was fundamentally human. Imam Husayn (as) is believed to have devised a plan for the revolution based on his convictions and material calculations in order to seize power. He attempted to execute his plan when he set out. However, he did not achieve his goals due to his misjudgment of the circumstances he faced, the determination of his enemies, and the betrayal of those who had invited him and pledged to support him. This eventually led to his and his companions' martyrdom and the failure of his project. Many eminent figures intellectuals had anticipated this outcome and had advised against his departure for this reason.

---

[41] "Both groups" is a reference to the Shia and Sunni schools of thought within Islam.

This perspective is prominent among many who discussed the events of Karbala.

PLANNING FOR THE RENAISSANCE AS DIVINE GUIDANCE

The second approach is that the planning for this event was divinely ordained. God, the Most High, entrusted Imam Husayn (as) with a mission that culminated in his martyrdom, the martyrdom of his companions, and all the tragedies and calamities that transpired. All of this suits the magnitude of this tragedy and its importance, guided by profound divine reasons known only to God. Some aspects of these wisdoms may have become apparent to us.

Imam Husayn (as) succeeded in his divine mission and achieved what he intended. Those who advised him against going out may not have been privy to the wisdom behind his actions. This is similar to how the wisdom behind the Treaty of Hudaybiyyah was hidden from Muslims, so they denounced it and blamed the Prophet (sawa) for it. Similarly, the wisdom behind Imam Hassan's (as) peace treaty with Muawiyah was not understood by some of the Imam's companions and others, so they denounced it. This is the case with many unseen matters where God's wisdom is hidden. Naturally, people are enemies of what they are ignorant of – and they may or may not be excused for their ignorance.

Since we, as Shia Muslims, believe in the immaculacy of Imam Husayn (as) and all the Imams (as), we are obliged to adopt the second interpretation for this blessed renaissance and all that has emanated from the Imams (as). Moreover, our traditions provide abundant evidence in which Prophet (sawa) and Imams

(As) affirm this interpretation. One such tradition is narrated by al-Umari from Imam al-Sadiq (as), stating:

إن الله عزّ وجلّ أنزل على نبيّه (ص) كتاباً قبل وفاته، فقال: يا محمّد
هذه وصيتك إلى النُّجَبَة من أهلك ... فدفعه النبيّ (ص) إلى أمير
المؤمنين (ع) وأمره أن يفكّ خاتماً منه ويعمل بما فيه، ففكّ أمير المؤمنين
(ع) خاتماً وعمل بما فيه، ثم دفعه إلى ابنه الحسن (ع)، ففكّ خاتماً منه
وعمل بما فيه، ثم دفعه إلى الحسين (ع)، ففكّ خاتماً فوجد فيه: أن
اخرج بقوم إلى الشهادة، فلا شهادة لهم إلا معك، واشترِ نفسك لله
عزّ وجلّ، ففعل، ثم دفعه إلى عليّ بن الحسين...

Allah, the Almighty and Glorious, sent a written message [with multiple seals] to His Prophet (sawa) before his death, saying: 'O Muhammad, this is your counsel to the chosen members of your family....' The Prophet (sawa) handed it over to the Commander of the Faithful (as) and ordered him to break a seal from it and act accordingly. The Commander of the Faithful (as) broke a seal and acted upon it, then passed it on to his son al-Hasan (as). He broke the seal from it and acted accordingly. He then passed it on to his al-Husayn (as), who broke the seal and found written: 'Go forth with a group to your martyrdom. Surely, they shall not be martyred except by your side. Ransom yourself for Allah, the Almighty and Glorious.' He followed the instructions, then passed it on to Ali ibn al-Husayn (as).... [42]

---

[42] *Al-Kafi*, 1:280.

In fact, we believe that the first interpretation is an injustice to the status of the Master of Martyrs (as) and trivializes the sanctity of his noble uprising. This belief is not solely based on our belief in his immaculacy or the traditions we have mentioned. Instead, it is based on two factors:

THE RENAISSANCE DID NOT ALIGN WITH MATERIAL VICTORY

The first factor is that the circumstances surrounding his blessed uprising and departure from Mecca to Iraq were not conducive to material victory. They required caution and deliberation, as evidenced by the unanimous advice given to him. Those who advised him presented him with matters that are not hidden from the awareness of many people, including Imam Husayn (as) himself. Thus, the determination of Imam Husayn (as) and his companions in embarking on this renaissance, along with the immense sacrifices that were required, must have had a different purpose than material victory.

HUSAYN'S (AS) KNOWLEDGE OF THE INEVITABLE DESTINY

The second factor is that the general Islamic history contains numerous accounts indicating that Imam Husayn (as) was well aware of his inevitable destiny, as were many others. There are many narrations that the Prophet (sawa), the Commander of the Faithful (as), and even Imam Husayn (as) himself have told about his martyrdom in this uprising. Indeed, details and specific events have been foretold and preparations were made for it.

Had Imam Husayn (as) not been destined for success in this mission, the Prophet (sawa) and the Commander of the

Faithful (as) would have warned him against it and prevented him from embarking on it. Imam Husayn (as) would never have contradicted them in this matter due to his well-known wisdom, faith, and piety.

Moreover, there are reports that indicate that they encouraged others to help him and admonished them not to abandon him.[43] However, there are no reports of them advising him not to go or preventing him from doing so.

There are also some anecdotes in the annals of history that bear witness to Imam Husayn's (as) unwavering determination to make sacrifices and his refusal to cling to the means of safety and peace. We cannot delve into the details of these accounts in this brief discussion.

---

[43] Ibn al-Athir wrote about Anas ibn al-Harith: "He was one of the companions of the Prophet (sawa) with noble qualities. Anas narrated, 'I heard the Messenger of Allah (sawa) while Imam Husayn (as) was on his lap, saying, "My son will be killed in a land known as Iraq. Whoever is present there should come to his aid."' Anas ibn al-Harith was killed alongside Husayn." Furthermore, the Commander of the Faithful (as) once said to Bara' ibn Azib: "O' Bara', will Husayn be killed, and you are alive, yet you do not come to his aid?" Bara' replied, "No, that will not happen, O' Commander of the Faithful." However, when Imam Husayn (as) was killed, Bara' used to mention this and say, "I deeply regret not being there to witness it and be killed alongside him." You can find these references in various historical sources such as: *Usd al-Ghaba*, 1:349; *Al-Bidaya wa'l-Nihaya*, 8:217; *Tarikh Dimashq*, 41:214; and *Sharh Nahj al-Balaghah* by Ibn Abi al-Hadid, 10:15.

We suffice with what Imam Husayn (as) expressed most
eloquently in his letter from Mecca to the remaining members
of the Hashimite family in Medina. He stated:

أما بعد فإن من لحق بي استشهد، ومن لم يلحق بي لم يدرك الفتح.
والسلام

> *Surely, whoever joins me will be martyred, and
> whoever does not join me will not attain victory.
> Peace.*[44]

This message underlines the Imam's firm resolve to sacrifice
himself for the cause.

---

[44] *Kamil al-Ziyarat*, 157; *Dalali'l al-Imamah*, 188.

THE GREATNESS OF IMAM HUSAYN

The greatness of Imam Husayn (as), his willingness to sacrifice, his unwavering determination, and his resolute spirit, shine. Those who make sacrifices typically hold onto the hope of safety and success in the project they plan to execute. When they begin executing and enter the battlefield, they may make mistakes or fail. At that point, their dignity and honor require them not to fall back in search for safety, but to persist until the end. Alternatively, they may unexpectedly find themselves in a battle without prior planning, and the pathways to success are blocked, but they still refuse to surrender, driven by their principles.

However, for a person to knowingly embark on a long-term project that inevitably ends in immense sacrifices and profound tragedies – and to plan for it with strength and determination – requires exceptional qualities.

When examining the details of the incident of Karbala objectively and fairly, it becomes clear that Imam Husayn (as) did not waiver from his decision to embark on this path and sacrifice his life. This was true from the moment he abstained from pledging allegiance in late Rajab and moved with his family and companions from Madina to Mecca, up until he gave the ultimate sacrifice along with his family members and

select companions – "the stars of this earth from the House of
Abdul Muttalib," as Lady Zaynab (as) described them. This was
followed by the looting of their belongings, the violation of
their sanctity, the captivity of their families, the defamation of
their characters, and leaving them as bait in the hands of
ruthless predators and wicked transgressors.

Despite all this, nothing deterred Imam Husayn (as) from his
determination, planning, persistence, and unwavering
commitment until the tragic end, which unfolded after nearly
six months.

All of this was due to his profound devotion to the Almighty.
His highest goal was to seek the satisfaction of God. He openly
expressed this in his noble sermon when he intended to leave
Mecca, saying:

خطّ الموتُ على ولدِ آدم مُخطّ القلادة على جيد الفتاة. وما أولهني إلى
أسلافي اشتياق يعقوب إلى يوسف. وخير لي مصرع أنا لاقيه. كأني
بأوصالي هذه تقطعها عسلان الفلوات بين النواويس وكربلا، فيملأن
منِّي أكْراشاً جوفاً وأجربة سبغاً. لا محيص من يوم خطّ بالقلم. رضا الله
رضانا أهل البيت. نصبر على بلائه ويوفينا أجور الصابرين...

*Death is to the son of Adam like a necklace is to the
neck of a young maiden. Oh, how I long for my
forefathers, like the longing of Jacob to Joseph. A fate
has been chosen for me that I will mee. It is as if my
limbs will be torn by desert wolves between Nawawis
and Karbala. They will fill their bellies [with my flesh]
and quench their thirst [with my blood]. There is no
escaping a day which has been written by the Pen [of
Divine Decree]. God's pleasure is our pleasure, the Ahl*

al-Bayt. We patiently endure His tribulations, and He
will surely grant us the rewards of the patient.[45]

What is striking in all of this is that Imam Husayn (as) managed
to choose for his sacred uprising individuals from his own
family and supporters who would not waver from his path, even
though they could have retreated at any time. They believed in
his leadership, surrendered to him with their last breaths, and
accepted their fate with profound insight, heightened joy, and a
sense of victory and happiness. They had unwavering faith in
his cause just as he did, so they clung to it and did not abandon
it even after he allowed them to leave and absolved them of
their allegiance. Even Imam Husayn's family (as) who
experienced horrors after his death; th3ere is no narration in
which any one of them denounced his noble position. Nor did
any of them complain as they followed him (as) till the
heartbreaking end. This is rare to happen without the care of
God and His support.

Researchers and intellectuals, including preachers and
conveyers of the message, should explore these aspects. They
should objectively and fairly investigate historical anecdotes
and perspectives, comparing them with the information
available to shed light on the truth and clarify it for the unaware
and the misled. All of this serves the truth and defends the
honor of the Master of Martyrs, Imam Husayn (as) – who,
despite his sacrifice, was treated unfairly by history. The same is
true of all the Ahl al-Bayt (as), their call, and their mission.

---

[45] *Kashf al-Ghummah*, 2:29.

AN INVITATION TO THE EDUCATED

It would be prudent for the educated to consider – additionally – the fruits of this blessed uprising and the significant gains it brought about, not only for Islam in general but specifically for the cause of the Ahl al-Bayt (as). These gains are indeed substantial.

This uprising came during the era of Imam Husayn (as), and so he was the one who executed it and not any other Imam (as). The Imams (as) are all equal in knowledge and courage, as has been narrated about them (as). They all emanated from the same light and followed the same path, even though their circumstances and experiences differed. Understanding this holds great importance in serving the cause of the Ahl al-Bayt (as) and gaining insight into their reality.

However, we cannot delve deeply into these matters here. Rather, we entrust them to researchers and truth seekers. We are willing to cooperate with them to the best of our abilities and within our circumstances.

We beseech Allah, the Exalted, to bestow success upon us and all the researchers to uncover the truth, to guide us in propagating it, and to increase our faith and submission. May He suffice us and all the believers against the wrongdoers and the mischief-makers. Indeed, He is the Most Merciful of the Merciful, the Best of Helpers, and He is sufficient for us.

Peace and blessings be upon you.

Muhammad Saeed Al-Tabatabai Al-Hakeem

24th of Dhu'l-Hijjah, 1424 H.

A MESSAGE TO THE VISITORS OF IMAM HUSAYN (AS) ON THE ARBAEEN

In the name of Allah, the Most Gracious, the Most Merciful

Praise be to Allah, the Lord of all worlds. Blessings and peace upon our master Muhammad and his pure and oppressed progeny. May the curse of Allah be upon all their enemies and oppressors until the Day of Judgment.

Peace and blessings be upon the supporters of Husayn (as) and his visitors.

For the first time, we have the opportunity to address you openly during your first procession, after the fall of the oppressive and tyrannical regime – a regime that pursued you during its long, dark era with killings, imprisonments, displacement, and oppression. They hoped to eliminate your procession and all your other commemorations, which are living manifestations of your loyalty to the Ahl al-Bayt (as), your connection with them, and your call to their noble principles and lofty teachings. They are a thunderous cry in the face of tyrants and oppressors, who lost their sleep and sanity over them.

The first caravan of righteous martyrs began almost thirty years ago, and more and more martyrs followed with astonishing determination and resolve. May Allah have mercy on those believing souls who strived for the sake of the truth of the Ahl al-Bayt (as) and the proclamation of their call. May He raise their ranks, unite them with their pure Imams, and gather them among their righteous supporters. He is the Most Merciful of the merciful.

Finally, that cursed nightmare has ended after a long period of darkness. As the great Lady Zaynab (as) said in her speech to Yazid:

فكد كيدك، واسع سعيك، وناصب جهدك، فوالله لا تمحو ذكرنا، ولا تميت وحينا، ولا تدرك أيامنا، ولا ترحض عنك عارها، وهل رأيك إلا فند، وأيامك إلا عدد، وجمعك إلا بدد، يوم يناد المنادي ألا لعنة الله على الظالمين

So plot as you wish. Continue with your undertakings. Exert all your efforts. But, by God, you will never erase our remembrance. You will never kill our inspiration. You will never reach our stature. You will never erase the shame of your undertaking. Indeed, your views are nothing but lies. Your days are numbered. Your armies will soon be disbanded. On that day, a caller will call, 'May God's damnation befall the wrongdoers!'[46]

The previous regime's hope to eliminate your procession and others like it has been in vain, just as the hope of tyrants and oppressors before him during long eras failed. They opposed these rituals and others like them, hoping to extinguish the fervor of faith that Imam Husayn (as) ignited with his blessed uprising. They wished to suppress the thunderous voice against

---

[46] *Bihar al-Anwar*, 45:135.

oppressors – a voice which affirms the words of Lady Zaynab (as) and Imam Sajjad (as) when they passed by those scattered bodies on the earth – a sight that would melt the hardest of hearts. Lady Zaynab (as) said:

وينصبون لهذا الطف علماً لقبر أبيك سيد الشهداء (عليه السلام) لا يدرس أثره، ولا يعفو رسمه، على كرور الليالي والأيام و ليجتهدن أئمة الكفر وأشياع الضلالة في محوه وتطميسه فلا يزداد أثره إلا ظهوراً وأمره إلا علواً.

And they will raise in this land a banner for the Master of Martyrs (as), whose effect will not be erased, and whose image will not fade, even after endless nights and days. The disbelieving leaders and followers of misguidance will strive to obliterate and obscure it, but it will only become more apparent, and its influence will only grow.[47]

So, praise be to Allah, and thanks to Him for His support to His servants, for fulfilling His promise to them. Congratulations to you for regaining your freedom in your procession towards the Master of Martyrs (as), your visit to him, renewing your allegiance to him, and fulfilling his rights.

How we wish we could share in that honor with you, but circumstances have prevented us from doing so. Nevertheless, these circumstances should not prevent us from drawing your attention to four important matters:

Firstly, observe gratitude to Allah for His blessings and all His favors, for He is the One who creates causes and defeats the

---

[47] Ibid, 45:180.

enemies. May your thankfulness to Him be put into practice by preserving the sanctity of these rituals, by obeying the commands of Allah and avoiding His prohibitions, by being cautious and verifying matters, and by adhering to the teachings of your Imams (as) in good conduct, righteous interactions, integrity of character, truthfulness in speech, and trustworthiness.

Secondly, let your procession and visit be a Husayni one, manifesting grief for the tragedy of the Master of Martyrs (as), cursing his killers, loyalty to the Ahl al-Bayt (as), confirmation of the injustice they faced, reminding others of their status and noble position, denouncing their enemies and those who wronged them, and emphasizing the crimes of those oppressors and usurpers. Do not let it deviate to something foreign to its essence, becoming a stage for promoting conflicting ideologies and slogans. Beware of those who exploit it for their interests and desires, for that would distort its true nature as intended by our Imams (as). Such deviation might lead to discord and conflicts that could justify its suppression or cause it to be marginalized or eliminated, as seen in past eras during some periods of internal strife.

Thirdly, you should adhere to the path of the Ahl al-Bayt (as) in upholding the truth, demonstrating sincerity in your actions, maintaining pure intentions, staying grounded in reality, and diligently verifying matters. You must collaborate with those who uphold the truth and the faith, those who harbor no doubts and are untainted by suspicions. Do not deviate from this path, allowing yourselves to be swayed by desires or deceived by flashy slogans and hollow calls.

وَالَّذِينَ كَفَرُوا أَعْمَالُهُمْ كَسَرَابٍ بِقِيعَةٍ يَحْسَبُهُ الظَّمْآنُ مَاءً حَتَّىٰ إِذَا جَاءَهُ لَمْ يَجِدْهُ شَيْئًا وَوَجَدَ اللَّهَ عِندَهُ فَوَفَّاهُ حِسَابَهُ ۗ وَاللَّهُ سَرِيعُ الْحِسَابِ

*As for the faithless, their works are like a mirage in a
plain, which the thirsty man supposes to be water.
When he comes to it, he finds it to be nothing; but there
he finds Allah, who will pay him his full account, and
Allah is swift at reckoning.*[48]

The path to truth and righteousness has been laid clear by
Allah, and He has not left His servants in ignorance.

Fourthly, you should foster unity, love, harmony, and empathy
among yourselves. Strengthen the bonds of brotherhood based
on the unity of your purpose, the nobility of your goal, and the
sanctity of your call. Even if there are differences in some
viewpoints, let your invitation be characterized by wisdom and
good counsel, and let it be marked by perfect calmness,
deliberation, and extreme caution against violence and
extremism, which can lead to hostility and conflict, yielding no
beneficial outcomes. Instead, they only bring harm and
disasters that have exhausted and weakened us.

We beseech Allah, the Most High, to aid you with His best
support, to guide you, accept your efforts, magnify your
rewards, answer your supplications, allow us to be a part of
your endeavors and righteous prayers, protect you from evil
and calamity, suffice you against your enemies, and rectify your
religious and worldly affairs. Indeed, He is the Most Merciful of
the merciful, the Guardian of the believers. He is Sufficient for
us, and He is the Best Disposer of affairs.

Peace and blessings be upon you.

Mohammad Saeed al-Tabatabai al-Hakeem (19 Safar 1424 AH)

---

[48] The Holy Quran, 24:39.

GUIDANCE TO THE STUDENT-PREACHERS OF THE ISLAMIC SEMINARY[49]

In the name of Allah, the Most Gracious, the Most Merciful.

Praise be to Allah, the Lord of all worlds, and blessings and peace upon our Master and Prophet, Muhammad, and upon his pure and noble family. May the curse of Allah be upon all their enemies until the Day of Judgment.

Peace and blessings be upon you.

Now, we find ourselves in the Islamic season of faith, a time overflowing with generosity, blessings, lessons, and admonitions. It is a time when we renew our allegiance, our covenant, our pledge, and our loyalty to the oppressed truth and its towering symbols in the realm of belief and action. In these days, we commemorate the tragic event of Karbala in its various dimensions. In this tragedy, we witness true servitude, submission, devotion, and obedience to Allah, as well as

---

[49] Abbreviated from the full original title: "Guidance from His Eminence Sayyid Al-Hakeem to the Student-Preachers of the Islamic Seminary on the Occasion of the Arrival of the Holy Month of Muharram, 1426 AH"

steadfastness on the word of truth, determination to stand up for noble goals, clear and noble intentions, staying true to principles, and maintaining a pure path through pure means. All of this, while avoiding ambiguity, deceit, and manipulation, and adhering to the highest moral values, clear vision, and keen insight. We see confidence in the results and that the outcome will be good, both in this world and the Hereafter. Then comes the ultimate sacrifice of one's dearest and most precious, even one's own life, in the way of Allah.

All of these virtues are embodied in the words and timeless stances of the Master of Martyrs, Imam Husayn (as), and in those who accompanied him on this journey. These virtues continue to overflow with life and illuminate the path for generations, even amidst the darkness of tribulations and the storms of upheavals.

Imam Husayn, peace be upon him, delivered a sermon in Mecca when he intended to depart for Iraq. He said,

خط الموت على ولد آدم مخط القلادة على جيد الفتاة ... كأني بأوصالي هذه تقطعها عسلان الفلوات بين النواويس وكربلاء ... رضا الله رضانا أهل البيت، نصبر على بلائه ويوفينا أجور الصابرين. لن تشذ عن رسول الله لحمته، بل هي مجموعة له في حضيرة القدس تقر بهم عينه وينجز بهم وعده. ألا ومن كان فينا باذلاً مهجته موطناً على لقاء الله نفسه فليرحل معنا، فإني راحل مصبحاً إن شاء الله تعالى

Death is to the son of Adam like a necklace is to the neck of a young maiden. […] It is as if my limbs will be torn by desert wolves between Nawawis and Karbala. […] God's pleasure is our pleasure, the Ahl al-Bayt. We patiently endure His tribulations, and He will surely grant us the rewards of the patient. The Messenger of God's (sawa) close kin will not deviate from him.

Rather, they will be gathered for him in Courtyard of Sanctity [in Paradise] – they will be the joy of his eyes and the fulfilment of his promise. Whoever would sacrifice his heart for us and is determined to meet God, let him journey with us for I am departing tomorrow morning God willing.[50]

In his will to his brother, Muhammad ibn Al-Hanafiyya, he said,

وإني لم أخرج أشراً ولا بطراً، ولا مفسداً ولا ظالماً، وإنما خرجت لطلب الإصلاح في أمة جدي (ص) أريد أن آمر بالمعروف وأنهى عن المنكر وأسير بسيرة جدي وأبي علي بن أبي طالب، فمن قبلني بقبول الحق فالله أولى بالحق، ومن ردّ عليّ هذا أصبر، حتى يقضي الله بيني وبين القوم وهو خير الحاكمين

I do not revolt due to discontent, nor out of arrogance. I did not rise as a corruptor, nor as an oppressor. Rather, I wish to call for reform in the nation of my grandfather (sawa). I wish to call for what is good, and to forbid what is evil. [I wish to] follow the tradition of my grandfather [the Prophet] and my father Imam Ali ibn Abi Talib. Whoever accepts me by accepting the truth, God is the best knower of the truth. Whoever rejects me, I shall be patient until God passes judgment between me and them. He is the best Judge.[51]

He wrote from Mecca, to his brother, saying,

---

[50] *Kashf al-Ghummah*, 2:239.

[51] *Bihar al-Anwar*, 44:329.

بسم الله الرحمن الرحيم من الحسين بن علي إلى محمد بن علي ومن قبله
من بني هاشم. أما بعد فإن من لحق بي استشهد، ومن لم يلحق بي لم
يدرك الفتح. والسلام

*In the name of Allah, the Most Gracious, the Most
Merciful. From Husayn ibn Ali to Muhammad ibn Ali,
and to those before him from the Hashimite family.
Surely, whoever accompanies me will be martyred, and
whoever does not accompany me will not witness the
triumph. Peace."*

When they reached Karbala, he addressed his companions in
his sermon, saying,

ألا ترون إلى الحق لا يعمل به والى الباطل لا يتناهى عنه، ليرغب
المؤمن في لقاء ربه، فإني لا أرى الموت إلا سعادة، والحياة مع الظالمين
إلا برما

*Do you not see that the truth is not acted upon, and
falsehood is not abandoned? The believer should yearn
to meet his Lord. Surely, I see death as nothing but
happiness, and life with oppressors as nothing but
disgrace.*

On the night of Ashura, he addressed his companions, and
allowed them to leave, saying,

هذا الليل قد غشيكم فاتخذوه جملًا ... فإن القوم إنما يطلبونني، ولو
أصابوني لذهلوا عن طلب غيري

*Night has shrouded you, so use it as your camel [i.e.
means of escape]. Our enemies do not want anyone but
me, and once they get to me, they would not want
anyone else.*

However, they strongly refused. On the day of Ashura, he addressed them, saying,

$$\text{إن الله تعالى أذن في قتلكم وقتلي في هذا اليوم فعليكم بالصبر والقتال}$$

Indeed, Allah the Almighty has allowed your killing and mine today. So, be patient and fight.

The tragedy unfolded with all its horrors, and the Master of Martyrs, peace be upon him, along with his family and companions, were martyred. Their bodies laid on the ground, beheaded and dismembered, in a brutal and savage manner that remains   a mark of falsehood and deviation. Those who remained from his family were then carried to Kufa. When they were about to leave Karbala, his sister, the Great Lady Zaynab (as), placed his noble body on her lap and raised it towards the sky, saying,

$$\text{إلهي تقبل منّا هذا القربان}$$

O' Allah, accept this sacrifice from us.

When they passed by the martyrs' bodies, Lady Zaynab (as) noticed her nephew, Imam Zain al-Abidin (as) with sadness and distress on his face. She tried to console him and spoke to him at length. She said,

$$\text{فوالله إن هذا العهد من الله إلى جدك وأبيك. ولقد أخذ الله ميثاق}$$
$$\text{أناس لا تعرفهم فراعنة هذه الأرض وهم معروفون في أهل السماوات}$$
$$\text{أنهم يجمعون هذه الأعضاء المقطعة والجسوم المضرجة فيوارونها}$$
$$\text{وينصبون بهذا الطف علماً لقبر أبيك سيد الشهداء لا يدرس أثره، ولا}$$
$$\text{يمحى رسمه، على كرور الليالي والأيام. وليجتهدن أئمة الكفر وأشياع}$$
$$\text{الضلالة في محوه وتطميسه، فلا يزداد أثره إلا علواً}$$

By Allah, this covenant is from Allah to your
grandfather and father. Indeed, Allah has taken a
pledge from a group of people – unknown to the
pharaohs of this land but known in the heavens – that
they will gather these severed limbs and bloodied
bodies, and bury them. They will raise a banner over
the grave of your father, the leader of the martyrs,
whose trace shall not be effaced, and whose mark shall
not be erased despite the passing of nights and days.
The leaders of disbelief and the followers of
misguidance will strive to erase and obliterate it, but it
will only increase in prominence.

When Ibn Ziyad asked her in Kufa, "What do you say about the
way Allah has treated the people of your house?", she replied,

ما رأيت إلا جميلًا، هؤلاء قوم كتب الله عليهم القتل فبرزوا إلى
مضاجعهم، وسيجمع الله بينك وبينهم فتحاج وتخاصم، فانظر لمن الفلج
يومئذ ثكلتك أمك يا ابن مرجانة

I saw nothing but beauty. These are men that God
decreed martyrdom for, so they went towards their
resting places. God will gather you and them, and you
shall be charged and proof will be set against you. You
will see who will fall on that Day. May your mother be
bereaved of you, O son of Marjana!

She said to Yazid when she delivered her speech in his court in
Damascus,

فكد كيدك واسع سعيك وناصب جهدك، فوالله لا تمحو ذكرنا ولا
تميت وحينا ولا يرحض عنك عارها. وهل رأيك إلا فند، وأيامك إلا
عدد، وجمعك إلا بدد، يوم ينادي المنادي: ألا لعنة الله على الظالمين

...

So plot as you wish. Continue with your undertakings.
Exert all your efforts. But, by God, you will never erase
our remembrance. You will never kill our inspiration.
You will never reach our stature. You will never erase
the shame of your undertaking. Indeed, your views are
nothing but lies. Your days are numbered. Your armies
will soon be disbanded. On that day, a caller will call,
'May God's damnation befall the wrongdoers!'

When Imam Zain al-Abidin (as) entered the city of Medina
along with the family of the Prophet (sawa), Ibrahim ibn Talha
asked, "Who is the victor?" The Imam replied,

إذا دخل وقت الصلاة فأذن وأقم تعرف الغالب

When the time for prayer comes, recite the calls the
Azan and Iqamah. That's when you will recognize the
victor.

We have recounted these texts and stances, which are just a few
examples among many, to remind ourselves of the sanctity and
objectives of this sacred uprising. Allah, in His wisdom,
ordained its eternal remembrance. It remains a call to the
conscience of the Ummah, awakening it from its slumber,
raising its morale, restoring confidence in itself, renewing its
faith, and reminding it of noble goals and virtuous qualities.

Allah, the Almighty, speaks the truth when He says,

ضَرَبَ اللهُ مَثَلًا كَلِمَةً طَيِّبَةً كَشَجَرَةٍ طَيِّبَةٍ أَصْلُهَا ثَابِتٌ وَفَرْعُهَا فِي
السَّمَاءِ* تُؤْتِي أُكُلَهَا كُلَّ حِينٍ بِإِذْنِ رَبِّهَا وَيَضْرِبُ اللهُ الأَمْثَالَ لِلنَّاسِ لَعَلَّهُمْ
يَتَذَكَّرُونَ

Allah presents an example: a good word like a good
tree, whose root is firmly fixed and its branches in the
sky. It produces its fruit all the time, by permission of its

Lord. And Allah presents examples for the people that perhaps they will be reminded.[52]

It is well known that there must be a conducive environment to embrace and nurture such a sacred cause, along with a group of faithful individuals who carry it forward and keep it alive. Indeed, Allah, the Almighty, created followers for the Ahl al-Bayt (as). They were formed from the virtuous essence of their lineage, mixed with the water of their allegiance. They rejoice in their joy and grieve in their sorrow. They responded to their call, carried it, interacted with it, protected it, and propagated it through sound reasoning. They engaged in continuous intellectual struggles against the false claims that spanned generations, with determination and sacrifice throughout their ordeal.

Each of the two camps had its distinctive features in terms of thought and behavior. Every type was consistent with its kind, and every vessel poured forth what it contained. Eternity, prominence, success, and prosperity belonged to the truth and its people, while disappointment, loss, retreat, and defeat befell the continuous claims of falsehood.

كَذَلِكَ يَضْرِبُ اللهُ الْحَقَّ وَالْبَاطِلَ فَأَمَّا الزَّبَدُ فَيَذْهَبُ جُفَاءً وَأَمَّا مَا يَنْفَعُ النَّاسَ فَيَمْكُثُ فِي الأَرْضِ كَذَلِكَ يَضْرِبُ اللهُ الأَمْثَالَ

That is how Allah compares truth and falsehood. As for the scum, it leaves as dross, and that which profits the people stays in the earth. That is how Allah draws comparisons.[53]

---

[52] The Holy Quran, 14:24-25.

[53] The Holy Quran, 13:17.

We have a great example of this in our present experience. Loyalty to the Ahl al-Bayt (as), sacrifice for their cause, rationality, ethics, determination, steadfastness, and passionate engagement are evident in the bitter struggle we face today against those who plot against the Ahl al-Bayt. They commit crimes, exhibit extremism, and display cruelty and brutality, even targeting women and children. And the situation has reached a point where some believers have sacrificed their precious lives for nothing other than their refusal to insult Imam Ali and Imam Husayn (as).

From this auspicious occasion, we must draw lessons and insights that aid us in our long and challenging journey. This is where the role of the speakers and preachers, may Allah guide them, comes into play. They should bear the responsibility and fulfill their duty in the following ways:

Firstly, they should attempt to present the event with its emotional and profound dimensions, filled with lessons and insights. They should connect with the rich cultural heritage associated with it, citing the words of Imam Husayn (as) and those who followed in his path. They should cite their positions that highlight the motivations behind this blessed resurgence and its principles, contrasting them with the statements and positions of the opposing side, which reflect their true nature and malevolent goals.

Secondly, they should emphasize the importance of loyalty to the Ahl al-Bayt (as) and the significance of adhering to them. They should underscore the impact of this allegiance on raising believers' morale and elevating their psychological, ethical, and cultural levels. This is most evident when taken in comparison with others. Ibn Abi al-Hadid, after expounding on the noble traits of Imam Ali (as), remarked, "These qualities have been passed down through the generations, from those who love and follow him to this day, just as the opposite traits of hostility, coarseness, and brutality have persisted on the other side. Anyone with the slightest knowledge of people's ethics and outcomes knows this."

This is reflected in Imam al-Hadi's (as) words in Ziyara al-Jami'ah,

وجعل صلاتنا عليكم وما خصنا به من ولايتكم طيباً لخلقنا وطهارة
لأنفسنا وتزكية لنا وكفارة لذنوبنا

He also decided our invocation of blessings upon you and our loyalty to you to be an excellence in our creation, a purity for our souls, a refinement of us, and a penance for our sins.

As Allah instructs us to say,

الْحَمْدُ لِلَّهِ الَّذِي هَدَانَا لِهَٰذَا وَمَا كُنَّا لِنَهْتَدِيَ لَوْلَا أَنْ هَدَانَا اللَّهُ

We praise Allah, Who guided us to this, for we would not have been guided if it were not for Allah guiding us.[54]

Thirdly, they should encourage believers to be grateful for Allah's continuous blessings in both their religion and worldly life. Gratitude is expressed through obedience to Allah, submission to His decrees, and adherence to His limits. This includes fulfilling religious obligations, avoiding sinful acts, speaking the truth, and maintaining trustworthiness. Believers should also embody the noble ethics of Islam. As the poet says:

---

[54] The Holy Quran, 7:43.

"For indeed, nations are but their morals, and if those are lost, they are lost."

May Allah extend His support and guidance to them. He is the best of supporters. As He says,

لَئِن شَكَرْتُمْ لَأَزِيدَنَّكُمْ ۖ وَلَئِن كَفَرْتُمْ إِنَّ عَذَابِي لَشَدِيدٌ

If you are grateful, I will certainly give you more. But if you are ungrateful, surely My punishment is severe.[55]

Fourthly, they should remind believers of their firm struggle against falsehood and the enemies' aggression, as well as the numerous risks surrounding them. They should urge them to unify their ranks, unite their voices, and stand firm on principles and general interests. In all aspects of their life, they should not put their trust except in those who deserve to be trusted, the ones of honesty and competence. They must be cautious of opportunists, troublemakers, and agitators. The path is long, and the struggle is harsh. In all of this, they should trust in Allah, seek His help, and rely on Him in all matters. Everything is in His hands, and all affairs return to Him. He is the Best of Helpers.

We pray to Him, the Most Merciful, and the Guardian of the believers. He is Sufficient for us, and He is the Best Disposer of affairs.

Peace and blessings be upon you.

Muhammad Saeed al-Tabatabai al-Hakeem

25 Dhu al-Hijjah 1425 AH

---

[55] The Holy Quran, 14:7.

QUESTIONS AND ANSWERS REGARDING THE HUSAYNI RITUALS

THE FIRST INQUIRY

In the name of Allah, the Most Gracious, the Most Merciful.

All praise is due to Allah, and blessings be upon Muhammad and his pure family.

His Eminence, the Grand Religious Authority, Ayatollah Sayyid Muhammad Saeed al-Hakeem, may his blessings continue.

Peace and mercy of Allah be upon you. After praying for your long life and complete well-being, I kindly request your guidance on the following questions:

1. In a previous response, you mentioned the permissibility of borrowing melodies from songs for use in eulogistic poems and elegies, and the permissibility of listening to such. Is this permissibility absolute, even if it leads to the degradation of Husayni poems, elegies, and religious eulogies due to the proliferation of musical styles and tunes that are familiar to those engaged in sinful acts? Furthermore, is it permissible for these borrowed melodies to be introduced into gatherings of remembrance and supplication or used in the settings of mourning and

condolence for the Master of Martyrs (as) and the rest of the pure Imams (as)?

Especially since some young people, when participating in the rituals of mourning and chest-beating, try to forget the words of the elegiac poem when they hear it set to a specific melody, and they secretly sing the original song lyrics associated with that melody.

It is worth noting that this trend of desecrating the sanctity of this important religious ritual and emptying it of its original content is steadily increasing. There are ongoing efforts to transform these elegies and poems into a state similar to songs in terms of melody, rhythm, and performance, except for the absence of musical instruments. This transformation involves changing the lyrics. Special artistic studios have been established in some countries to produce elegies, chest-beating rituals, and eulogies that are prepared and recited within highly equipped studios with modern audio technology. These recitations often include various melodies and are later distributed in the markets.

If the ruling is indeed permissibility, could consideration be given to studying it as a secondary matter, taking into account the possibility of the intrusion of frivolity and lightness into the sacred gatherings due to the inclusion of various musical styles and tunes in Husayni and religious poems? This could lead the ritual to deviate from its lofty objectives and fail to fulfill its noble function.

2. In a previous response, it was also mentioned that listening to film soundtracks, which usually accompany movie scenes, is permissible. Does this ruling of permissibility apply to all types of film soundtracks, taken in a general

sense, even though film soundtracks encompass various genres and styles depending on the different films, their scenes, and the diversity of their content? Some soundtracks are associated with scenes of combat, chase, nature, fear, or nostalgia, while others are linked to love and romance scenes, for example, where the soundtrack may be in harmony with the theme and, in itself, be stimulating or entertaining. Does the previous ruling of permissibility include all these cases?

3. In some of your honorable responses, you mentioned the terms "conceptual doubt" (shubhah mafhumiyyah) and "factual doubt" (shubhah mawdu'iyyah). Given that most believers are unfamiliar with the meanings of these two terms, let alone the distinction between them, could you please clarify these concepts as an introduction to the application of religious rulings for the obligated individuals?

We are deeply grateful and hold you in the highest esteem, and we kindly request that you do not forget us in your blessed prayers. We eagerly await your ongoing guidance and supplications. Peace and mercy of Allah be upon you.

Riyadh Abdul Sahib al-Mousawi

9 Safar 1423 AH

RESPONSE TO THE FIRST INQUIRY

In the name of Allah, the Most Gracious, the Most Merciful, and all praise is due to Him.

1. The mentioned ruling is based on the observation of the subject matter itself. As for considering the ruling as a secondary matter, there are no set limits or restrictions. The application of secondary rulings varies depending on

individuals and their convictions. Therefore, we cannot delve into these details. Such a discussion will not be fruitful due to the differences in subjective understanding, especially if there is financial benefit for some individuals, which may lead them to attempt to defend their interests. This can lead to debates and disputes with dubious consequences.

It is preferable for those who wish to serve this great ritual to focus on calm persuasion to guide the believers towards what is better and more appropriate for its objectives, without resorting to harshness or agitation. It is even more beneficial for knowledgeable individuals to promote and disseminate mournful rituals that adhere to the purpose of this rite, avoiding foreign elements that do not align with its goals or compromise its sanctity. Announcing and advocating for this approach, believers, with their loyalty and solid foundations in grief and tears, will recognize what is more suitable and closer to the reality of this ritual. They will encourage and promote it, sidelining other practices until their appeal diminishes, their market deteriorates, and their advocates abandon them. This should be done without resorting to harshness or agitation that might increase an individual's determination to adhere to their convictions and zealously defend and promote them. We ask Allah, the Most High, to unite the believers in the service of these objectives.

2. The answer is specific to film soundtracks that are not associated with entertainment or stimulation, or that do not contain elements of either. Otherwise, they are considered forbidden.

3. Conceptual doubt arises when there is a general doubt about the general meaning and concept of a legal subject matter. For example, if one hesitates between whether the

concept of "just" is applied to someone who avoids major sins only, or whether it is someone who avoids all sins including minor ones. Similarly, if there is doubt about the concept of "intoxication," whether it refers to the loss of reason or extends to any form of exhilaration or elation beyond the conventional. Another example is doubt regarding the concept of "daytime," whether it means the appearance of the dawn's light or specifically the rising of the sun, and so on. In such cases, it is necessary to refer to the knowledgeable jurist to determine the legal concept and then act accordingly.

Factual doubt, on the other hand, arises when there is doubt about external factors while the legal concept of the subject matter is clear. For instance, there may be doubt about whether a person committed major sins such as withholding the rights of others or neglecting prayers, and therefore there is doubt whether the label of "just" applies. Or there may be doubt about whether a specific liquid is an "intoxicant" in accordance to any assumed definition. Or if one were to doubt whether the current time is dawn or whether the sun had risen, and so on. In such instances, one is not required to refer to a jurist; instead, the responsibility falls upon the individual to discern based on their own knowledge or other reasonable legal means.

After this explanation, it is quite challenging to clearly differentiate between the meanings of conceptual doubt and factual doubt, especially in the context of music and singing, in the written form, such that it is easily understood by the questioner and all readers. Therefore, we have refrained from elaborating on their meanings and have focused on stating their rulings. This is to encourage the questioner to seek verbal clarification, enabling a suitable explanation of the distinction that aligns with their intellectual and cultural level.

We ask Allah, the Most High, to grant you success and guidance.

Peace and blessings be upon you.

Mohammad Saeed al-Tabatabai al-Hakeem

9 Jumada al-Awwal 1423 AH

THE SECOND INQUIRY

Esteemed Grand Ayatollah, Sayyid Muhammad Saeed al-Tabatabai al-Hakeem,

Peace, mercy, and blessings of Allah be upon you. After placing our trust in Allah, we have resolved to produce an epic international narrative film that portrays the timeless event of the Tragedy of Karbala, showcasing the high Islamic values and grand principles for which Imam al-Husayn (as) sacrificed his life. On this occasion, we do not intend to depict Imam al-Husayn (as) in a visual format that closely resembles the features of ordinary humans. Instead, through cinematography, direction, and lighting, his character will be presented as luminous, devoid of the usual human traits, more akin to a vision.

Before we embark on this endeavor, we seek your guidance regarding the ideal Islamic portrayal of Imam al-Husayn (as) in the film. We would like to know if our proposed approach is correct or not, and we welcome your advice and opinion on this matter.

Please provide us with your guidance and insights, and may you be rewarded. May Allah protect and support you.

Mohammad Saeed al-Taraihi

12 Rabi' al-Thani 1418 AH

RESPONSE TO THE SECOND INQUIRY

In the name of Allah, the Most gracious, the Most Merciful. All praise is due to Him.

After considering your noble intentions and earnest efforts to serve the Ahl al-Bayt (as) and spread their sublime principles for which they sacrificed so dearly, we would like to draw your attention to the following:

1. It is essential to avoid presenting sacred personalities, such as Imam al-Husayn (as), with specific and clearly defined features. Simply adding luminosity to an actor, with distinct human [facial] traits, is insufficient. Yes, the film can symbolize and allude to him (as).

2. Emphasize the oppression suffered by Imam al-Husayn (as) by first establishing his right. Then, highlight the magnitude of the tragedies and hardships endured by him and his family, many of which were heinous and unnecessary – only caused by the perpetrators' lack of humanity and immense criminality.

3. Focus on the fact that Imam al-Husayn (as) was fully aware of his impending martyrdom before embarking on his journey. This is evident from his speech in the Grand Mosque of Mecca a day before his departure, his conversations with Ibn Abbas and Ibn al-Hanafiyya, his letter to Muslim ibn Aqil (as), his determination to continue the march after learning of Muslim's martyrdom, and his maneuvering with al-Hurr al-Riyahi until he was forced to a particular location by Ibn Ziyad. Additionally, his letter to the Hashimites of Medina, in which he informed them that those who follow him will be martyred, and those who do not will not achieve the triumph, reinforces this notion. He also said in his conversation with ibn Sa'ad that this is a solemn covenant [given by Allah], and so on. This is in addition to the clear prophecies that have been narrated from Prophet (sawa), the Commander of the Faithful (as), and others about Imam Husayn's (as) murder. This helps affirm that his sacrifice was for a noble purpose he successfully accomplished, not the result of a

leader's failed plan or miscalculations, as some adversaries may claim.

4. Highlight the exemplary aspects of his life (as) and the lives of those with him. Demonstrate that they were fully aware of their mission. They were sure that the outcome in the hereafter will be good and had confidence in the success of their endeavors. Provide evidence through their statements and actions that supports this.

5. Emphasize the necessity of this tragic uprising alongside the greatness of the sanctities that were violated and the horror of the events that transpired. This is to awaken the conscience of the Ummah to the oppression of the rulers who focused on the legitimacy and holiness of their rule as caliphs. Through this, they attempted to legitimize their deeds and decrees, claiming them to be religiously binding, even when they contradicted Islamic laws derived from the Quran and the Sunnah. Such actions would lead to the decline and oblivion of religion, as seen in previous religions. Therefore, the heinous violation of sanctities and brutality of the massacre at Karbala had the most profound impact on alerting the Ummah to the reality of rulers, removing their holiness, stripping their actions of legitimacy, and divorcing them from religion. It showed their true reality, represented by crimes and oppression, and prevented them from distorting the religion.

6. Highlight the supernatural aspects related to the event, such as its premonition, cosmic signs preceding it, the speech of Imam Husayn's severed head (as), and other extraordinary occurrences that transcend natural laws. These should serve to underscore that this was a divine epic destined by Allah for significant purposes and benefits in promoting religion and faith, and affirming the word of Allah on earth.

7. It might be beneficial to screen the film when it is done to a group of renowned scholars and experts for their feedback before releasing it to the public. Our office in the holy city of Qom is at your disposal for any possible collaboration to ensure the success of this honorable endeavor.

In conclusion, we pray to Allah, the Most High, for your success and guidance in serving the principles of the Ahl al-Bayt (as) and spreading their message for posterity in this world and the Hereafter.

Peace, mercy, and blessings of Allah be upon you.

Muhammad Saeed al-Tabatabai al-Hakeem

13 Jumada al-Thani 1418 AH

THE THIRD INQUIRY

In the name of Allah, the Most Compassionate, the Most Merciful.

To the esteemed Grand Ayatollah Sayyid Muhammad Saeed al-Hakeem (may Allah prolong his life),

I kindly request your guidance on the permissibility of composing elegiac poems (*qasa'id*) in the form of *lisan al-hal*[56] of the Imams (as), Lady Zaynab (al-Hawraa) (as), or the companions of Imam Husayn (as) regarding the tragedy of Karbala, as per the narrations we have. We, the poets of the Husayni tradition, have been confronted with this religious dilemma, which has affected our poetic production in the service of the Ahl al-Bayt (as). Please provide us with your esteemed opinion in accordance with Islamic jurisprudence.

Poet, Basim al-Ward al-Kadhimi

23 Safar 1421 AH

RESPONSE TO THE THIRD INQUIRY

In the name of Allah, the Most Gracious, the Most Merciful. All praise is due to Him.

The writing, composition, and recitation of such elegiac poems (*qasa'id*) are among the best and most noble of deeds. The Imams (as) have encouraged the writing and recitation of

---

[56] *Lisan al-hal*, or "the language of the situation," is a poetic form in which the poet describes what the Imam, or anyone in his position, might have said. A concern arises of whether this form of expression is confused to be the actual words of the historical figure in question, as opposed to a poetic expression. -eds.

poetry about them (as) and emphasized its importance. They have mentioned a great reward and immense recompense for it, and we cannot examine all that in detail here.

The misunderstanding may have arisen from the misconception that this poetry involves lying or falsehood because the Imams (as) did not utter the exact words mentioned in the poetry. However, there is no basis for this claim because lying involves contradicting reality through a specific claim. In other words, lying occurs when the speaker intends to convey something that does not correspond to the truth. However, this does not apply in this context, as the poet's intention is not to report actual words spoken, but to convey a message or sentiment by using a poetic form of expression and imagery created for that purpose.

Humans are capable of inventing and imagining whatever they wish in order to serve the purpose of emphasizing an event to the listener or reader. Therefore, the allegation that the poetry mentioned contains lies or falsehood does not hold. Rather, it is a legitimate form of expression that falls within the realm of artistic and poetic creativity.

Such was the habit of the poets and the well-spoken across all arts and different time periods. For example, the poet of Ahl al-Bayt, Sayyid Haydar al-Hilli speaks to himself and says, "He said to it [i.e., himself], 'Hold fast to honor for an honorable soul is the best adornment.'"

He also said about the companions of Imam al-Husayn (as) and their courage, "They leveled its hills and said to it, kneeling, 'We will take the hills' place.'"

Sayyid Ja'far al-Hilli also said about them, "The enemy wanted to humiliate them, but their spears said, 'It would be easier to reach the stars!'"

And there is much more.

Predating all of this is a poem that narrations say was recited by Imam al-Hadi (as) in the courtyard of the Abbasid Caliph al-Mutawakkil:

> They slept atop the mountains, guarded by
>
> Strong men – but the mountains did not avail them
> […]
>
> They were called by a caller after their passing,
>
> 'Where are the beds, crowns, and jewelry?
>
> Where are the pampered faces that were
>
> Veiled by mantles and drapes?'
>
> But the grave answered those questions instead –
>
> 'These are their faces, being fought over by maggots!'

It is also narrated that the Commander of the Faithful (as) eulogized Lady Zahraa (as) by saying,

> Why have I stood over graves,
>
> greeting the grave of my beloved –
>
> but to no response?
>
> My beloved! Why do you not answer us?
>
> Have you forgotten the companionship
>
> Of your loved ones?
>
> But the beloved said,
>
> 'How can I answer you when I am
>
> A prisoner to stones and dirt?'

He also said in a sermon about Paradise,

*[Paradise] continued to display itself to your past and
bygone nations.*

Clearly, Paradise cannot speak or display itself. However, he is
illustrating the reality through creative imagery.

Let's also consider the verses from the Quran,

$$ثُمَّ اسْتَوَىٰ إِلَى السَّمَاءِ وَهِيَ دُخَانٌ فَقَالَ لَهَا وَلِلْأَرْضِ ائْتِيَا طَوْعًا أَوْ كَرْهًا قَالَتَا أَتَيْنَا طَائِعِينَ$$

*Then He directed Himself to the sky while it was smoke
and said to it and to the earth, 'Come [into being],
willingly or by compulsion.' They said, 'We have come
willingly.'[57]*

And the statement of Allah, the Almighty,

$$يَوْمَ نَقُولُ لِجَهَنَّمَ هَلِ امْتَلَأْتِ وَتَقُولُ هَلْ مِن مَّزِيدٍ$$

*The Day when We will say to Hell, 'Have you been
filled?' and it will say, 'Are there some more?'[58]*

It is very possible that the intention behind these verses is not to
narrate actual conversations between Allah, the Earth, the Sky,
and Hell. Instead, it could be a form of expressing the state of
affairs or the message using a style of imagery created for that
purpose, aiming to emphasize the matter being presented and
to captivate the listener without the need for a literal
interpretation.

Thus, there is no basis for the doubt raised regarding the
permissibility of such expressions. There is no room for

---

[57] The Holy Quran, 41:11.

[58] The Holy Quran, 50:30.

considering them as lies or falsehoods. On the contrary, composing poetry and reciting it in honor of the Ahl al-Bayt (as) is recommended. The poet is free to choose the mode of expression and invent imagery to effectively convey the noble cause being presented to the audience, stirring their emotions and fostering loyalty to the Ahl al-Bayt (as).

We pray to Allah, the Most High, to grant you success in serving the principles of the Ahl al-Bayt (as), in instilling their values in the hearts of believers, in inspiring them to recite and pledge loyalty to them, in embodying their noble virtues, and in calling others to truth and goodness with wisdom and good counsel.

Peace and blessings be upon you.

Mohammad Saeed al-Tabatabai Al-Hakeem

24 Rabi' al-Awwal 1421 AH

THE FOURTH INQUIRY

In the name of Allah, the Most Gracious, the Most Merciful.

Your Eminence, the Grand Ayatollah, Sayyid Muhammad Saeed al-Hakeem,

What is your opinion regarding the mourning rituals of Imam Husayn (as) that are observed in countries around the world during the days of Ashura, using the traditional methods and practices that have been customary in our country? These rituals include spreading black banners, providing water to participants, offering food, conducting mourning processions in various forms, holding gatherings for condolence, and engaging in chest-beating (*latm*).

We are in dire need of your guidance, and to you belongs the reward and recompense [from Allah].

Sayyid Murtada Muhsin al-Sindi

RESPONSE TO THE FOURTH INQUIRY

In the name of Allah, the Most Gracious, the Most Merciful.

Praise be to Allah, the Lord of all worlds, and peace and blessings upon our master Muhammad (sawa) and his pure family (as). May Allah's curse be upon all their enemies until the Day of Judgment.

We approve and strongly endorse the implementation of the rituals in the way mentioned, for several reasons:

Firstly, when we refer to the narrations of the Imams (as) and observe their positions – as well as the position of the Shia during their time – we conclude that they have acknowledged and praised these rituals. They encouraged them and highlighted the great rewards in store for those who uphold them in the eyes of Allah (swt) and the Imams (as).

Secondly, these rituals have proven their effectiveness and significance throughout history. They serve as a means of uniting the hearts of believers and fostering their commitment to the true principles of the Ahl al-Bayt (as). They evoke strong emotions and dedication, leading individuals to sacrifice their most prized possessions. They are the pillars of the true call and its impenetrable fortress, whose support never ceases. The forces of evil are not idle in trying to eliminate them and silence them. Thus, rooting this call within their hearts and drawing them to it is one of the most important reasons for its survival and emergence.

Furthermore, there is a greater need for the expatriates to hold fast to these rituals on account of two main reasons:

Firstly, these rituals remind them of their authentic roots and make them cherish the positive aspects of their homeland, strengthening their connection to it and preventing them from feeling alienated in their new societies.

Secondly, because of their uniqueness in those societies, these rituals draws the attention of people to the call of truth. This may motivate them to inquire about it, study its reality, and eventually come to believe in it. This is especially true considering our limited means of communication throughout history, or the absence of such means in most circumstances.

However, it is crucial to emphasize two points:

Firstly, these rituals should be carried out alongside adhering to all religious teachings, such as performing the obligatory acts and avoiding forbidden actions. This will align the individual with the true objectives of Imam Husayn's (as) uprising, and allow them to follow the path of the Imams from the Ahl al-Bayt (as). These rituals should serve as a platform for conveying the true call of Islam and fostering love and devotion towards it.

Secondly, these rituals should be conducted in a manner that does not disturb others who are unfamiliar with them and ensures that they are not inconvenienced. We should show kindness to others and live alongside them in harmony. In this way, there will be a lower likelihood that others will become averse to these rituals or to those who practice them. This approach may allow them to reflect on this invitation and its reality. Perhaps God Almighty will even make it a source of blessings and mercy for them.

Some might think that the contemporary developments in the world require the evolution of the methods of propagation and that rituals should be replaced with what aligns with the current reality. We approve of these attempts to find new means suitable to the developments of the contemporary world. However, this should be accompanied by maintaining these traditional rituals as they are, not replacing them.

When these rituals first came into existence, they seemed strange in the context of their time and faced the harshest forms of resistance, ridicule, and mockery. However, they remained steadfast, asserting themselves against that reality and fulfilling their function in the best possible way. Just as their strangeness did not hinder them in the past, it should not hinder them in the present with the help of Allah Almighty.

May Allah grant those responsible for these rituals guidance and success in their endeavors, bless their efforts, guide them on the right path, accept their deeds, and make their work a source of blessings and mercy in both their religion and worldly affairs. May He also include us in the reward for their efforts, for 'those who love a people's action will be with them as partners in it.'

Peace and blessings be upon you.

Muhammad Saeed al-Tabatabai al-Hakeem

15 Dhul-Qa'dah 1443 AH

THE FIFTH INQUIRY

In the name of Allah, the Most Gracious, the Most Merciful.

His Eminence, the Grand Religious Authority, Ayatollah Sayyid Mohammad Saeed al-Tabatabai al-Hakeem,

Peace and blessings be upon you.

In the past, an inquiry was made to His Eminence, the Late Grand Jurist, Ayatollah Sheikh Mirza Mohammad Husayn Al-Na'ini (may Allah elevate his status in Paradise) regarding the rituals associated with Imam Husayn. He responded as follows:

> In the name of Allah, the Most Gracious, the Most Merciful,
>
> To Basra and its surroundings,
>
> Peace and blessings be upon our esteemed brothers, the honorable residents of the Basra region.
>
> We have received your letters and inquiries in eastern Karrada concerning the ruling on mourning processions and related matters. With God's blessings we have returned to the Holy City of Najaf safely. We now provide answers to these questions by clarifying the following points:
>
> 1. The processions of mourning (known as *mawakib*) taking place in the streets and roads on the tenth of Muharram (*Ashura*) and similar occasions, is permissible and favored. It is considered one of the most prominent ways to hold the commemoration of the oppressed [Imam], and to convey the message of the Husayn (as) to all those near and far. However, it is necessary to maintain the sanctity of this noble ritual and avoid anything

inappropriate for such a worship – such as singing or use of instruments of [musical] amusement. The residents of different neighborhoods must also avoid pushing and shoving to attempt to proceed one another, and the like. If any of these prohibited actions occur, it is forbidden (*haram*). However, the prohibition of such actions does not extend to the mourning procession itself, and it remains valid. This is like someone looking at a woman during the prayer; [the act itself may be forbidden but] it does not invalidate the prayer.

2. There is no objection to the permissibility of *latm* (striking oneself) with hands on the cheeks and chests to the extent of causing redness and bruising on the body. Furthermore, striking with chains on the shoulders and back to the extent that causes redness or bruising is also permissible. Moreover, if both *latm* and striking lead to the emergence of a small amount of blood due to the strong force applied, it is still permissible.

    As for drawing blood from the forelock using swords or knives, it is considered permissible as long as it is considered safe. Blood must be drawn without causing damage to the skull, it must not lead to losing enough blood to cause harm, and so forth. This is known by experienced individuals who are familiar with the technique of striking rituals.

    If the act is practiced according to what is commonly accepted as safe, but incidentally, the amount of blood drawn becomes excessive, it does not render the act impermissible. This is analogous to someone who performs ablution, takes a bath, or fasts believing these actions are safe, but later realizes that they are harmful [in their specific circumstance].

However, it is preferable – indeed, more cautious – not to let those who are not knowledgeable and experienced engage in such practices. This is especially true for young people who do not consider the consequences they bring upon themselves due to the magnitude of the tragedy and the fullness of their hearts with love for Imam Husayn (as). May Allah firmly establish them in this world and the Hereafter.

3. It appears that there is no objection to the permissibility of using theatrical reenactments and representations that have been traditionally employed by Twelver Shia Muslims for centuries to conduct rituals of mourning, weeping, and lamentation. This may include men wearing women's clothing, provided that it is done within the context of such representations. Although there may have been initial reservations about its permissibility, upon further review, it has become clear that what is considered impermissible is when a man completely departs from male attire and fully adopts female clothing without changing back to his original attire. This is not the case in these representations. This clarification has been recently added to our commentary on "al-Urwat al-Wuthqa."

It is necessary to ensure that these representations are also free from any violations of Islamic law. However, even if these violations are present in some instances, this does not extend the prohibition to the act of representation itself, as mentioned earlier.

4. The drum, known as *dammam*, used in these processions – as long as its usage is primarily for mourning, calling for gatherings, signaling horseback riding, or during cultural expressions, and not used for activities that involve entertainment and joy, as is commonly known in Najaf Al-Ashraf – appears to be permissible. Allah knows best.

5th of Rabi' Al-Awwal, 1345 Hijri

Drafted by the humble,

Mohammad Husayn al-Gharawi al-Na'ini

This fatwa has been presented to the esteemed authorities and scholars of our nation, may Allah have mercy on those who have passed and prolong the life of those who remain. They have provided valuable comments on this matter.

Therefore, we kindly request your esteemed opinion and commentary on this issue in accordance with your perspective and knowledge, in service to the true doctrine. We ask Allah, the Most High, to encompass you with His care and the care of the Master of the Age and Time, Imam Al-Mahdi (as), to bring about his relief and victory. Peace and blessings be upon you.

Sheikh Muhammad Kan'an

Judge of the Jaafari Court in Beirut

20 Rajab 1425 AH

RESPONSE TO THE FIFTH INQUIRY

In the name of Allah, the Most Gracious, the Most Merciful.

All praise is due to Allah, the Lord of all worlds. Blessings and peace be upon our master Muhammad (sawa) and his pure and virtuous family (as). May Allah's curse be upon all their enemies until the Day of Judgment.

Peace be upon you, and may the mercy and blessings of Allah be upon you. We beseech Allah, the Most High, to grant you support and guidance in serving the religion and benefiting the believers. May He bestow upon you safety, happiness, and well-being in this world and the Hereafter.

What our esteemed scholar has mentioned in his detailed response is of the utmost quality and soundness. It is, in our view, unquestionably appropriate. Our religious verdict aligns with it, as well as the consensus of many scholars of our sect, including our esteemed teachers and others – may Allah elevate their status and reward them greatly for their contributions to this sect.

Indeed, there is no doubt about the importance of emphasizing these matters. They have the greatest impact in reminding people of the tragedies of the Ahl al-Bayt (as) and stirring their grief. This leads to increased devotion to the Ahl al-Bayt, growing love and affection for them, firm commitment to their guardianship, acknowledgment of their leadership, distancing from their enemies and oppressors, and avoidance of those who oppose them and harbor animosity towards them.

This is one of the most significant religious objectives, as it strengthens the bonds of faith – including love for the sake of Allah and aversion for the sake of Allah, loyalty to His chosen servants, and enmity towards His adversaries. These concepts are well-supported in the narrations of both sects – Shia and Sunni.

Moreover, the following two points deserve further attention:

Firstly, people vary in how they express their emotions in connection to the events related to Ahl al-Bayt (as), whether they are occasions of joy or sorrow. Each group of people has its own way of expression that aligns with their understanding, feelings, and environment. If they were forced to adopt a different approach, it might not resonate with them and they may not engage with it effectively. This could cause the emotional connection to fade over time, resulting in the loss of the ability to express feelings and emotions toward the event.

It is necessary, therefore, to allow each group the freedom to choose the method that suits them in expressing their emotions – so long as it remains within the boundaries of what is permissible. Prohibiting their preferred expressions and imposing a different approach could diminish their emotional engagement and passion for the event.

Secondly, history and experiences have shown that those who bear the banner of the true call and its hardships are the common masses of the believers. They persevere through obstacles, problems, troubles, and risks. Because of their sheer numbers, they are not easy to eliminate by the adversaries of this call. Their efforts cannot be halted, their mission cannot be stifled, and they cannot be manipulated with enticement. In contrast, the intellectual class – such as religious scholars and public intellectuals – play a vital role in guiding and nurturing the followers of the call, protecting it from distortion and misrepresentation. Nevertheless, on their own, they may be vulnerable to elimination or diversion from the call. Only the common masses – the majority of believers – are the true fortress for both the call and those who carry its banner.

Therefore, it is essential to empower the masses to express their emotions in the manner they choose during various religious occasions. Encouraging them to do so allows their emotions to deepen and spread among them. This enables them to continue their mission relentlessly and with determination, serving as a source of strength during crises. Their strength will endure even when the intellectual class faces pressures that might paralyze them, rendering them incapable of even signaling or hinting at their true feelings. The recent events in Iraq provide a poignant lesson in this regard.

This is what we wanted to emphasize in this brief statement. There are other aspects related to the topic that we have discussed previously or can address at a later time.

We beseech Allah, the Most High, to grant success to all in what He loves and is pleased with, and to support them with guidance and assistance. He is the Most Merciful of the merciful, the Guardian of the believers, and He suffices us. What an excellent guardian and helper He is.

Peace be upon you, and may the mercy and blessings of Allah be upon you.

Mohammad Saeed al-Tabatabai al-Hakeem

27th of the blessed month, 1425 AH

THE SIXTH INQUIRY

In the name of Allah, the Most Gracious, the Most Merciful.

His Eminence, the Grand Religious Authority, Ayatollah Sayyid Mohammad Saeed al-Tabatabai al-Hakeem,

After greetings and further prayers, we request answers to the following questions, and may you remain supported by Allah.

1. Is it not *makruh* (disliked) for the one offering prayers to wear black clothing? How can we reconcile this religious ruling with the belief that wearing black is recommended as a sign of mourning for Imam Husayn (as)?

2. In your esteemed opinion, which of the *maqatil*[59] is most highly regarded?

3. Some people tie threads and or pieces of fabric on the pulpit of the Husayniyyah (a congregation hall used for mourning rituals) or the banners raised therein. Others express their willingness to purchase these items in search of blessings and healing. Is it permissible to sell these items and use the proceeds for Husayni mourning ceremonies, for example?

4. Some fatwas condition the permissibility of particular acts or Husayni rituals on the condition that they do not 'weaken' or 'harm' the religion or school of thought. What is the criterion for determining whether certain acts are 'weakening' or 'harmful'?

Kazim al-Bahadli

---

[59] The *maqatil* is a category of books that relay the tragic events that befell the Ahl al-Bayt (as) throughout history, especially the tragedy of Karbala.

4th of Rabi' al-Thani, 1423 AH

RESPONSE TO THE SIXTH INQUIRY

In the name of Allah, the Most Gracious, the Most Merciful, all praise is due to Him.

In response to your first question, combining these two rulings is not difficult, especially given the prevalence of primary rulings being limited or overridden by secondary rulings in certain situations. For instance, the *karahah* (disapproval) of wearing black may be alleviated if it becomes more suitable for one's health. Similarly, the *istihbab* (recommendation) to wear white may be overruled if it proves detrimental to one's health or if it becomes a symbol for enemies of the faith. Choosing to break one's *mustahab* (recommended) fast in response to a believer's invitation could be deemed superior to continuing the fast. And so on.

Wearing black as an expression of mourning is an established practice. Add to that the fact that it is *mustahab* (recommended) to show grief and sorrow over the tragedy of Imam Husayn (as). The same is true of all the tragedies within our religious tradition that have been commemorated over generations stemming back to the eras of the immaculate Imams (as). Given all this, it is sufficient proof to overcome the notion of wearing black as *makruh* (disliked).

Additionally, there is a prominent narration from Umar, son of Imam Ali ibn al-Husayn (Zayn al-Abidin) (as), where he said,

لما قتل الحسين بن علي صلوات الله عليه لبس نساء بني هاشم السواد والمسوح، وكنّ لا يشتكين من حرّ ولا برد، وكان علي بن الحسين يعمل لهنّ الطعام للمأتم

When al-Husayn ibn Ali (as) was martyred, the
women of Banu Hashim wore black and observed
mourning without a complaint of heat or cold. Ali ibn
al-Husayn (as) himself prepared food for them during
the mourning rituals.

This narration suggests that Imam Zayn al-Abidin (as)
approved of the women's dressing in black during their
mourning. This is contrary to the reports stating that wearing of
black is disliked, both as a general rule as well as specifically
during mourning for the deceased.

Another exception is made for Imam Husayn (as) when it
comes to *latm* (beating of the chest or face) in the act of
lamentation. Khalid ibn Sudayr narrates that Imam Al-Sadiq
(as) said,

ولا شيء في اللطم على الخدود سوى الاستغفار والتوبة، ولقد شققن
الجيوب ولطمن الخدود الفاطميات على الحسين بن علي. وعلى مثله
تلطم الخدود وتشق الجيوب

There is no penance for beating the cheeks [in
lamentation] except seeking forgiveness and repentance.
[The exception is that] clothes were torn, and the cheeks
were struck in lamentation by the Fatimi women for
Husayn ibn Ali (as). Indeed, for his sake, cheeks are
rightly struck and clothes are [rightly] torn.

All of this is because grieving for Imam Husayn (as) is not an
objection to divine decree and destiny ordained by God – such
objection is detestable in religious law. Rather, it is grief for the
religion itself, where its laws were violated and its sanctities and
symbols desecrated. It is a condemnation of the wrongdoers
who perpetrated these acts.

In response to your second question, since most of the narrations of the *maqatil* are *mursal*[60] reports, relying on them is due to the lofty personality of the author of each in terms of their knowledge and reliability in transmission. Examples include Shaykh al-Saduq's *al-Amali*, Ibn Tawus's *al-Luhuf*, and Ibn Nama's *Muthir al-Ahzan*. In addition, some contemporary scholars have compiled works that trace the events back to the sources from which they were derived. Examples of such works are the writings of the Abd al-Razzaq al-Muqarram and Sayyid Mahdi Bahr al-Uloom. In such cases, the preference for a particular narration is based on the importance of the source it originates from.

In this discussion, two important points should be noted:

One, most accounts of historical events are *mursal* or mentioned with weak chains of narration. If we were to disregard these accounts, very little historical information would remain, as we have mentioned in some of our previous responses to seminary students and scholars. It is not wise to rely solely on what is written by mainstream historians like Tabari and Ibn al-Athir, and disregard what our righteous scholars (may their pure souls be sanctified) have written. Rather, a comprehensive comparison between the two sides should lead to the opposite conclusion. Our scholars have been more concerned with the truth, following the guidance of their Imams (as), and they are more likely to maintain objectivity in accordance with their noble etiquette. Historians from other

---

[60] *Mursal* is a technical term that refers to narrations or hirstorical reports in which one or more of the narrators in its chain are not specified, resulting in a break in the chain of transmission.

factions, on the other hand, have tried to obscure, conceal, or distort truths.

Indeed, it is beneficial to refer to what mainstream historians mention when it contradicts their own worldview and supports the narrative of the Ahl al-Bayt (as). In such cases, their mention of these events confirms their clarity and the fact that they are well-known, even if it goes against their own worldview and desires.

Two, the absence of a specific source for a narration does not necessarily make it false. In earlier times, numerous books were written about the martyrdom of Imam Husayn (as), relying on narrations from eyewitnesses of the events or the teachings of the Imams of the Ahl al-Bayt (as) during their lifetimes. They diligently conveyed the tragedy, its sorrows, calamities, lessons, and moral values. If these books have been lost to us, it is very likely that their content has persisted in the collective memory of people, passed down from one generation to the next, or transmitted in a somewhat informal manner in some later texts that have reached us.

Furthermore, many events may not have been formally recorded but have been transmitted orally among people in successive generations until they reached us through oral transmission, even if without a specific source. This possibility is sufficient to allow us to use these accounts in support of established fact or to discourage a clear falsehood. This aligns with what we have mentioned in some of our responses appended to the mentioned message.

In response to your third question, the sale of the mentioned fabrics is problematic due to the seller not having ownership of them and the lack of clear authority over them. Consequently, the one who has placed them has abandoned them, so they can be given out for free. However, it is permissible for the recipient to give some money as a voluntary donation to support the mourning rituals without it being considered a payment for what they received.

In response to your fourth question, 'weakening' and 'harm' to the religion are self-evident concepts that do not require elaboration. Yes, their applicability and occurrence may vary depending on different viewpoints, locations, times, and circumstances. It is not feasible for us to provide a universal standard for this.

May peace and blessings be upon you.

Mohammad Saeed al-Tabatabai al-Hakeem

23 Jumada al-awwal, 1423 AH

THE SEVENTH INQUIRY

In the name of Allah, the Most Gracious, the Most Merciful. To His Eminence Grand Ayatollah Sayyid Muhammad Saeed al-Hakeem (may Allah prolong his life), what is the ruling on the act of *tatbir*,[61] striking oneself with chains, and the use of other recognized symbols of mourning for Imam Husayn (as) within Shia communities, especially in light of the media campaign against it?

RESPONSE TO THE SEVENTH INQUIRY

In the name of Allah, the Most Gracious, the Most Merciful, and all praise is due to Him.

Tatbir and similar expressions of grief, such as flagellation or the use of other mourning symbols, are rituals that promote Islamic principles and manifest one's emotions for this purpose. As such, they are considered religiously desirable. However, there may be cases where they are prohibited due to secondary reasons, such as causing prohibited harm either individually or collectively. No universal standard can be given for this, as the factors affecting the ruling vary by time, place, and circumstances. Thus, opinions on the matter may differ among scholars. We pray to Allah, the Almighty, for guidance in this regard for all believers. Indeed, He is sufficient for us, and He is the best disposer of affairs.

We would also like to point out the following:

---

[61] Tatbir is a mourning ritual where an incision is made on the head and blood is allowed to flow over the individual's head, face, and body as a show of grief for the massacre of Karbala.

First, the media campaign mentioned in the question does not revolve around the perceived repulsiveness of *tatbir*, but rather stems from other motives. There are customs, practices, and rituals outside the Shia community that can be equally, if not more, repulsive. Yet, the media tends to downplay or ignore them, instead focusing on any negative portrayal of the Shia community. Thus, if Shia Muslims cease the practice of *tatbir*, they will still be subject to false accusations and unjust vilification by a prejudiced media. The intention here is not to excuse the media's biased behavior but to highlight the fact that abstaining from *tatbir* will not necessarily change this situation. Shia Muslims have been and continue to be the target of oppression and discrimination as long as they adhere to the principles of truth and justice, revealing the wrongdoings of the oppressors and falsehoods of the deceitful.

Second, the denunciation and attacks on *tatbir* and similar practices are veiled attempts to denounce and attack the Shia due to their beliefs and practices. They wish to denounce the Shia to the world because of their continued practice of these rituals. Therefore, for Shia to engage in similar attacks on these rituals is inexcusable defeatism and only serves to aid their oppressors. Those who believe *tatbir* to be forbidden should clarify that this is the case due to secondary reasons, and is therefore temporary and contingent on circumstances. Holding such a view should not mean attacking those who do not see it as forbidden because those specific secondary reasons do not apply. The Shia must apply mutual respect in areas of difference in opinion.

This perspective will maintain the integrity of the religious ruling within its rightful boundaries. Shia Muslims have always upheld their religious principles with dignity, which has been a source of pride for them and an illuminating emblem of their allegiance to the true path of faith. May Allah support their call and raise it for all to hear.

Moreover, this perspective will serve to preserve the unity of the Shia community and avoid discord and conflict among its members – especially in these times, when unity is desperately needed.

In my belief, this fierce attack against Shia Islam in relation to *tatbir* and other practices will only end in one of two ways. It could end with the Shia compromising on their principles and bargaining over them, which – God willing – will not occur.

Alternatively, it could end through the continued patience and resilience of the Shia community. This is not for the sake of *tatbir* and the similar practices, which are only secondary matters where opinions could differ. Rather, it is for the sake of their true beliefs which they convey with wisdom and good advice. They will make clear the honorable and true nature of their faith, expose the evil oppressors, and silence the rabid slanderers. After all:

كَتَبَ اللَّهُ لَأَغْلِبَنَّ أَنَا وَرُسُلِي ۚ إِنَّ اللَّهَ قَوِيٌّ عَزِيزٌ

Allah has written, 'I will surely prevail, I and My messengers.' Indeed, Allah is Powerful and Exalted in Might.[62]

Peace and blessings be upon you.

Mohammad Saeed al-Tabatabai al-Hakeem

---

[62] The Holy Quran, 58:21.